THE ENNEAGRAM WORKBOOK

Understanding Yourself & Others

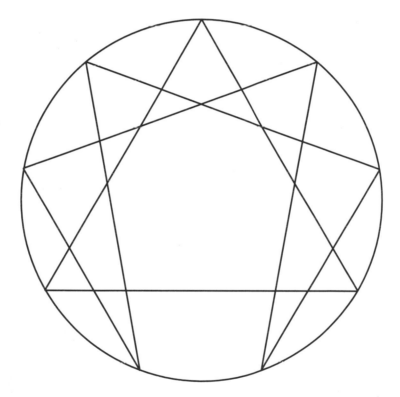

KLAUS VOLLMAR

Sterling Publishing Co., Inc.
New York

"I wonder if I am waking—
it's just there is so much to do
when I am tired of sleeping."
  —Susan Vega

Library of Congress Cataloging in Publication Data Available

Published 1998 by Sterling Publishing Company, Inc.
387 Park Avenue South, New York, N.Y. 10016
Originally published in Germany by Kailash, an imprint of Heinrich
Hugendubel Verlag under the title *Das Arbeitsbuch zum Enneagramm*
Copyright © 1994 by Klausbernd Vollmar
English translation © 1998 by Sterling Publishing Co., Inc.
Distributed in Canada by Sterling Publishing
℅ Canadian Manda Group, One Atlantic Avenue, Suite 105
Toronto, Ontario, Canada M6K 3E7
Distributed in Great Britain and Europe by Cassell PLC
Wellington House, 125 Strand, London WC2R 0BB, England
Distributed in Australia by Capricorn Link (Australia) Pty Ltd.
P.O. Box 6651, Baulkham Hills, Business Centre, NSW 2153, Australia
Manufactured in the United States of America
All rights reserved

Sterling ISBN 0-8069-0323-6

Contents

1. The Enneagram: A Cosmic Symbol

"We think of the Enneagram simply as an intelligent summary of an insight into the function of the universe." —Anthony G. E. Blake

The Enneagram as an Archetype

As a child, I found it exciting to occupy myself with patterns and diagrams, which I filled in with color crayons. Today I still begin every longer text with a diagram. This book was created from such a diagram, which hung on the wall while I was writing and led the flow of my thoughts.

I believe that all people think in diagrams and patterns. Playing around with different diagrams to bring my thoughts into order, I realize that I have understood the facts correctly only when I can present them in an aesthetically satisfying diagram.

With such patterns and diagrams as the Enneagram, we move to the level of the archetypes. On this level, form takes precedence over content. The Swiss psychologist Carl Gustav Jung (1875–1961) often stressed in his work that it was a misunderstanding to believe that archetypes were determined by content. He wrote:

> It must be pointed out once again that archetypes are determined not by content but by form, and the latter only in a very restricted way. An original image, determined by its content, can be proven only when it is filled consciously with the material of conscious experience. Its form, on the other hand, is ... to be compared approximately with the workings of a crystal, which, in a manner of speaking, pre-forms the crystal structure in the mother-lye, without itself owning a material existence.[1]

It seems to me that the basis of our thinking is to be found in geometric patterns and forms. That's why, in classical antiquity, the Greeks considered geometry one of the most important disciplines for self-knowledge.

In this book, I want to present a very special diagram. With its help, not only self-knowledge, but also knowledge of the world and of the entire universe can be structured. The diagram of the Enneagram was introduced into spiritual discussion by the Armenian wisdom teacher George Ivanovitch Gurdjieff (1865–1949). For me, the Enneagram represents a type of archetypal pattern that stimulates imaginative images and can be used as a map for our consciousness.

The Enneagram—A Movable Diagram

What especially fascinates me about the Enneagram is its openness or mobility. As Jung explains in the quote above, the original image of the archetype is filled with content—conscious experience. In the same way, the Enneagram is filled with content, depending on which level of consciousness you are on.

It is said that when two people who do not know each other meet in the desert, and each one draws an Enneagram in the sand, it is—depending on the content of the Enneagram—possible to recognize which person is the more developed.

This story, which is very popular in Gurdjieff circles, shows that you can fill the Enneagram with your knowledge. I will suggest only a few possibilities and hope to stimulate you to arrive at your own creative way of dealing with this cosmic symbol. Of course, first you need to understand how to fill the Enneagram with content, and then you can go on to make your own allocations to the individual Enneagram points.

Unfortunately, the Enneagram has recently been seen mainly as a rigid structure for different character types. But that is only one level of the Enneagram. Above this level, many much more interesting levels construct themselves, which reflect social and economic processes. Here the Enneagram begins to move; it begins to dance. According to Gurdjieff, the Enneagram can be understood correctly only when you can imagine it in motion.

The dynamics of the Enneagram can also be seen in combination with the individual Enneagram points. In the last analysis, every point of the Enneagram can be connected with every other point. From this results a diversity of personality types, showing the steps of a process that I will describe in detail in the chapter "The Dynamics of the Model."

Gurdjieff or Ichazo?

George Ivanovitch Gurdjieff and Oscar Ichazo, two important teachers of this century—about whom we will often talk in this book—are considered the two "fathers of the Enneagram."

Gurdjieff would probably turn over in his grave at the way the Enneagram is viewed here. Access to his teachings was supposed to be made as difficult as possible so that they could be approached only with strenuous effort. In this workbook, I try to make it all easy to digest. An unsystematic thinker, Gurdjieff sometimes changed his system, left many aspects of it incomplete, and often only hinted at his meanings. He never explained the Enneagram completely in his work. It was the task of his pupils to work out his teachings precisely; and I have taken on that task with this book.

In the same way, Ichazo would feel misunderstood in this workbook, since I flavor his teachings of personality types (which are not exactly original) with some salt and pepper and Gurdjieffian spiciness.

The strength of the Enneagram does not lie in personality "types." That, for me, is only a by-product of Enneagram study, though a very useful and practical one.

As a result, I am caught between two stools. Though it is uncomfortable, it is an extremely common position among Gurdjieff pupils because, as his grandmother said, "Never do anything the way other people do it!" Only that way, I believe, is knowledge possible.

We can still feel the influence of Gurdjieff wherever the Enneagram is used. I want to follow in his tracks, and also in those of Ichazo, even though it is difficult to combine their different views of life. But it is worth the effort. The Enneagram becomes more lively and clear when viewed from both its origins.

Many people are shocked, in their Enneagram studies, that in the description of the nine types as described by Ichazo and his successors, the negative and the shadow come to the fore. There, clearly, Gurdjieff's disposition still shines through. Completely contrary to today's fashion in spiritual circles, Gurdjieff stressed the negative side of the human being. When people viewed themselves in this way, Gurdjieff believed they would be unable to continue fooling themselves constantly, and at the same time, would develop the motivation to do serious work on themselves.

The teaching of personality types helps us to go beyond the limited style of observing our own ego, in order to reach a more comprehensive understanding of our existence. That is how the contemporary American psychotherapist Margaret Frings Keyes, and many other followers of the teaching of types, express it. This is exactly what Gurdjieff tried to do with his use of the Enneagram—escape from one's own ego to arrive at a cosmic understanding of the personality. Nevertheless, there is no mention of personality types from Gurdjieff. Among other things, Gurdjieff focused on the "essential trait," which he considered to be self-deception. This deception, caused by wishful thinking, impedes work on oneself. Ichazo, probably inspired by this concept, came to his teaching of personality types, which is based on a self-deception that the individual considers "his character." With that, Ichazo is very close to Freud's student Wilhelm Reich (1897–1957), who strove for a softening of the hardened human character armor.

Since in spiritual circles the Enneagram is consumed like fast food, I want to help it to be viewed with pragmatic depth again. I want to share the excitement of it with you, show you how you can become friends with the multifarious Enneagram, and use it.

You have probably already assumed that I am coming from the Gurdjieff doctrine—a doctrine into which one can project a lot of bite and self-will. But as a teacher and psychotherapist, I also admire Ichazo's clearly conceived personality types, which I use as a psychological tool. Here, I intend to convey the full meaning of the Enneagram, because I am disappointed at how superficially it is often used. It deserves better!

The Enneagram is as complex and paradoxical as human life itself. Perhaps that is what fascinates me so much and why I want to convey it to you playfully, easily, and sometimes with a twinkle in my eye—but along with exercises that will help you in a practical way.

Hints on How to Use This Book

This book teaches you the language of the Enneagram as if it were a foreign language, but without the performance pressure of formal lessons. In an entertaining way, you will be introduced to the meaning and grammar of the Enneagram. But in order to really understand this language, you need to use the Enneagram continually. Suddenly, a new

world of undreamed of references and meanings will open up for you. This book wants to help you achieve this experience. Just enter into the text, and the world of the Enneagram will embrace you.

*   *   *   *

Each chapter of this book can be read by itself and in random sequence, entirely as you wish. I recommend that you try all the exercises at least once, because you need to understand the Enneagram not only with your head but in practice, which the exercises provide. According to Gurdjieff, real thinking does not take place in the head—but in the heart.

The first chapter of this book deals with the sources of the Enneagram. The positions of Gurdjieff and Ichazo are important here, because they were the first to apply scientific concepts to it. In this chapter you will find:

- information about the history of the Enneagram

- the presentation of the positions of Gurdjieff and Ichazo

- the philosophical backgrounds of the Enneagram.

The second chapter describes the Enneagram as a general pattern of order. It leads you into the world of personality types and examines the Enneagram as a symbol that clarifies cosmic connections. This chapter tells you what the Enneagram can explain and in which fields you can apply it. And the most popular question—how to find your personal Enneagram type—is answered as you take various tests.

Furthermore, in this chapter, the central exercise for self-remembering—the basis of Gurdjieff's consciousness work—is described in detail. Here you find:

- Enneagram type tests and a critique of those tests

- ways to use the Enneagram to examine processes of all kinds

- Enneagram connections to the chakras

- Enneagram connections to the order of colors

- Enneagram connections to astronomy and astrology.

The third chapter asks you to take a ruler and compass and draw regular and irregular nine-star figures. This brings you to the Enneagram via geometry, through which you will come to learn the mathematical secrets of the Enneagram and the special role of the number Nine in different cultures. You will find:

- mathematical and geometric references to the Enneagram

- a variety of drawing exercises

- information about the number Nine

- comparisons between the Enneagram and the Kabbala.

In the fourth chapter, I describe the nine points of the Enneagram systematically. You can also use this chapter as a reference book for the different aspects of the Enneagram points. Each Enneagram point is broken down as follows:

- a general description of the Enneagram point

- a description of the process it symbolizes—social, economic, personal

- its general strength and weakness

- the allocation of the chakras to the Enneagram points.

- the allocation of colors to the Enneagram points

- cosmological allocations to the Enneagram points from astronomy and astrology

- symbols for the Enneagram points—animals, countries, famous personalities

- an overview of the different Enneagram allocations

- key questions regarding each Enneagram point.

The fourth chapter describes the rather static basic structure of the model in detail.

The fifth chapter looks at the dynamics of the model. You will learn about the two different movement directions in the Enneagram, their stress and relief points, and the combinations of the Enneagram points.

Each stress and relief point is broken down systematically as follows:

- the perspective in a process

- characteristics of the point

- what flows from the original point

- what flows from the new point

- the consequence of this movement.

Each of the 33 different combinations of individual Enneagram points is presented in a way that will clarify the following aspects:

- factors increasing strength at the two points

- factors that contradict each other at the two points

- the result of this connection

- the frequency with which it occurs.

The sixth chapter consists of a collection of different exercises that use different senses and bring you new approaches, so that you can experience the Enneagram from different viewpoints.

Most of these exercises can be practiced often. If you do this, they will always lead to a new result.

The final chapter combines Ichazo's personality types with Gurdjieff's process model, and so provides a theoretical summary of the book.

2. Where Does the Enneagram Come From?

Gurdjieff and His Sources

The Armenian teacher George Ivanovitch Gurdjieff presented the Enneagram for the first time publicly in 1916 in his St. Petersburg study group. The Enneagram then became the basis of his system of teaching. Gurdjieff said that the Enneagram contained his entire doctrine in compressed form. He stressed that this system was used only by his teaching system. Before him, the Enneagram was taught in no esoteric school. Despite its importance, we are surprised not to find it in any of Gurdjieff's books directly—although indirectly we find it in all his publications.

For Gurdjieff and his successors, work with this symbol was bound up with group work and practical work. Exploring the Enneagram meant to experiment and learn by dealing with the cosmic symbol. Also, Gurdjieff was continually learning new things as he dealt with the Enneagram, and altering his presentation of it. Gurdjieff himself worked with it specifically in his "Movements."

Definition of "Movements"

Many followers of Gurdjieff believe that the body exercises or holy dances called "Movements" are at the core of Gurdjieff's teachings. They consist of more than 100 very complicated, mostly counter-rotating body Movements that are intended to help the student develop greater consciousness. In these Movements not only do the different body parts move with the music, but, also, some-times against its rhythm. At the same time, the student has to adjust to the movements of the other dancers and coordinate with them. "According to Gurdjieff, complicated word and number sequences were added, which were either thought silently or spoken out loud. Furthermore, the student had to perceive parts of his body in a certain sequence and activate certain feelings." [2]

The students who participated in the Movements as dancers or spectators immediately realized that the Movements conveyed Gurdjieff's vision of human beings and their position in the cosmos. The Movements are based for the most part on the Enneagram, as they describe the outside of the figure. At the same time, the dancers tried to interpret the laws of the Enneagram through their bodies. For that purpose, certain exercises in concentration were helpful. These Movements were kept so secret that they have never become accessible to the general public until now. Those movements taught in the Sannyasin movement Oshos (formerly Baghwan) are a poor imitation of Gurdjieff's Movements.

The Movements or "holy dances" convey to the student the rhythm and the phases of processes in a non-verbal way. Students in these classes often reported that it was through the Movements that they learned to know the Enneagram physically. Their bodies became able to perceive the point at which a process needed a new energy push from the outside to keep going—the so-called shock point in the Enneagram, which I'll refer to later. I myself experienced a deeper understanding of the Enneagram through these strangely difficult body movements, which were sometimes disparagingly called "holy gymnastics."

Gurdjieff indicates in his autobiographical teaching novel, *Meetings with Remarkable Men*, that his source for the Enneagram and the Movements was the Sufis and the legendary Sarmoun Brotherhood, which supposedly flourished in Babylon around 2,500 years B.C. This Sarmoun Brotherhood is mentioned only once in Gurdjieff's entire esoteric literature, and is thought to be a symbol of a school of wisdom or for the "inner teacher." This becomes clear through the description of the main cloister of this brotherhood, in which symbols appear everywhere, and which is often used to characterize the place of spiritual insight and voice.

According to the Gurdjieff student John Godolphin Bennett (1897–1974), the Sarmoun Brotherhood dates back to the scholarly Achaldan Society from Atlantis, which Gurdjieff brings up frequently in his main work, *Beelzebub's Tales to His Grandson*, as a model for the correct conduct of life. The reference to this Atlantean society, though, does not bring us further historical explanation, because quite obviously it too is a symbol.

If Gurdjieff did take over the Enneagram from some esoteric group, then it seems likely it would have been the Sufi order of the Naqshbandi. This order, with which Gurdjieff probably had contact, falls back on not only Arabian, but also on Babylonian and Mesopotamian, number symbolism. In these systems, the number Nine plays a prominent role.

On one hand, the Enneagram is reminiscent of the Mandala, as it is presented in Tibetan Buddhism, representing a map of the inner worlds of the human being and, at the same time, the cosmos. Gurdjieff visited Tibet as an agent of the Russian Czar in 1897, where he undoubtedly saw Mandalas. In Tibetan shamanism also the number Nine is important. For example, the shaman gives nine sacrifices for the nine dangers and after that enters into a transaction with nine sisters, the witches of the underworld, who are supposed to help him find the soul who has lost its way or been abducted. In their rituals, Tibetan and Nepalese shamans even today protect themselves with nine bells made from iron, and nine sun and nine moon symbols.

Furthermore, Gurdjieff had well-founded knowledge of the spiritual systems of the Egyptians. In Egyptian mythology, the world creator and original god Atum, who was especially revered in Heliopolis, plays an important role. In the pyramid texts, he appears as the first principle that arose from chaos. This god is depicted as being self-absorbed and masturbatory. He swallows his own semen, which he spits out and from which the nine principles of creation are formed. These nine principles can be compared with the nine points of the Enneagram, as illustrated by the basic principles of each process.

In another variation of the Egyptian creation myth, the four elements appeared in pairs, springing out from the womb of the Big Mother, Ma-Nu. Together with the force of the Big Mother and the nine basic principles or Enneades, the earth was created. The Enneades also represent the oldest and most important gods of Egypt.

In Germanic mythology, though Gurdjieff did not know it well, the number Nine is also of great importance. For example, Odin hangs for nine windy nights in a tree where he learns nine magic charms (the runes). I mention this only briefly, in order to show that the magical significance of the number Nine is archetypal. This can be traced back, probably, to the nine body openings of the human being.

At a closer look, it appears that the number Nine also represents a symbol of perfection. In German mythology, for example, Heimdall, as a child of nine mothers, stands for an image of the human being in its entirety, and Odin's nine charms symbolize perfect knowledge.

So the Enneagram, which requires nine steps for the completion and perfection of a process, fits right in with the Germanic, the Greek (the nine Muses, daughters of Zeus, protected the perfection of the spirit in art and science), the Chinese (the nine-step pagoda is thought the symbol of perfection), the Babylonian, and the Chaldean uses of the number Nine.

Starting in 1916, the Enneagram was brought closer to a small circle of followers that included Peter Demian[ovitch] Ouspensky (1878–1947), John Godolphin Bennett, and Ivan B. Popoff. They made the Enneagram known to a larger group of Gurdjieff students of the Fourth Way, mostly through publications. The first extensive information about the Enneagram can be found in Ouspensky's book *In Search of the Miraculous*.[3]

Ichazo and His Successors

Oscar Ichazo, born in 1930, states that he had taken over the psychological personality types of the Enneagram from Sufi teachers in the Pamir (Afghanistan). But that was about 40 years after Gurdjieff first mentioned the Enneagram. The assumption that Ichazo "copied" the Enneagram from Gurdjieff does not seem unreasonable, especially since he never wanted to mention his teacher. From Gurdjieff's point of view, Ichazo watered down the Enneagram, degrading it from a cosmological model to an easily manageable study of personality types.

Ichazo worked with the Enneagram in Chile in the Arica Institute from about 1970 on, and in its subsidiary in the U.S. (in New York), which was founded in 1971. From the Arica Institute, the teaching of personality types traveled through humanistic psychologist Claudio Naranjo to the Esalen Institute (California), where the Jesuit father Robert Ochs of Loyola University took it on and spread it with vehemence and great success in ecclesiastical circles. (Gurdjieff remarked at the beginning of the 20th century that he hoped the Pope would one day read his work, and if the Jesuits continue to spread the Enneagram with such conviction, that day won't be far off.) The Enneagram then made its way from humanistic psychology via the Jesuits to the entire ecclesiastical community.

The American Franciscan friar Richard Rohr played an essential role in Germany as an agent of the Jesuit tradition. He collaborated with the Bavarian Lutheran pastor Andreas Ebert, to publish in 1989 a Christian Enneagram book, in which almost nothing is left of Gurdjieff's thought.

Eli Jaxon-Bear, who published a psychological Enneagram book at the same time, is also an important figure in the development of the personality types tradition of humanistic psychology.

The Difference Between Gurdjieff and Ichazo in the Use of the Enneagram

With his teaching of the Enneagram, Gurdjieff follows the traditional course of self-knowledge through a teacher. Without having an authorized teacher and being a member of a study group, you cannot, according to Gurdjieff, work with the Enneagram properly, since only a group can develop the right understanding of the Enneagram in its members. Gurdjieff's approach to the Enneagram is bound up with the "Work." Work, in the Gurdjieffian sense, means work on oneself in a study group in order to wake up from one's usual state, which is sleep, and achieve greater consciousness and increasing clarity. For Gurdjieff and his successors, working with the Enneagram is much more significant than it is for Ichazo and his successors. The Enneagram is viewed by Gurdjieff and other teachers of the so-called Fourth Way as a cosmological model, which, like the zodiac in astrology, depicts the laws of our cosmos.

In the tradition of Ichazo and the Jesuits, the Enneagram is considered only as a psychological model of a dynamic teaching of personality types. In dealing with this model, instruction through a teacher is not absolutely necessary. Here the Enneagram reveals simply nine equal types, formed through the programming of reactions and viewpoints, not based upon each other in any sense as a path to enlightenment.

Definition of a Path to Enlightenment

By a path to enlightenment I mean a path from the unconscious mechanical human being to the conscious individual.

Ironically, one of the differences between Gurdjieff's and the religious approach to the Enneagram is that Gurdjieff stresses the entire general and spiritual character of the symbol, whereas the religious viewpoint focuses only on the psychotherapeutic aspect.

While Gurdjieff and the schools of the Fourth Way are directed toward consciousness training and the recognition of cosmological connections, the ecclesiastical Enneagram users work towards psychological knowledge of oneself and others. Nevertheless, both paths lead to the same goal—consciously serving the creation of harmony in the cosmos. What is for the one group the *Work*, is for the other group the *community work*. The goal is the same, but the method is completely different.

Schools of the Fourth Way

- The Enneagram is a symbol of cosmic connections.

- It has to do with processes of all kinds.

- It symbolizes, among other things, a path to enlightenment. Dealing with the Enneagram is spiritual training.

Ichazo and the Religious Tradition

- The Enneagram is a symbol for the different human types, a recognition of socialized viewpoints and reactions.

- Dealing with the Enneagram lets us recognize ourselves and others more precisely.

Parallels Between Gurdjieff and Ichazo

Despite all the differences mentioned here between Gurdjieff and Ichazo, there are also parallels between the two.

It is striking that both Gurdjieff and Ichazo were very secretive about their teachers. The psychologist and psychic Helen Palmer[4] believes that Gurdjieff knew the personality types of the Enneagram and used them in his work, but because he did not find his students developed enough to accept this information, he withheld it from them.

This opinion, which is widespread among American psychologists, finds its support in the fact that Gurdjieff assumed that human beings suffer needlessly because of a dark spot in their character. Everyone is hampered through his "false personality" (as Gurdjieff called this dark spot). The Enneagram, as a model, shows nine different types of false personality. If we can recognize our false personality through self-observation, as Gurdjieff taught it, then we are capable of living up to our full potential. The knowledge of the false personality, reflected by the nine Enneagram types, puts us in a position to dissolve it and thus to undertake the most important step towards the Work with our higher consciousness.

Gurdjieff, in his gruff way, used to recognize everyone's false personality immediately, and then pick on it continually. By doing that, he intended to destroy the so-called "buffers"—"defense mechanisms" in Freudian terminology. (It is interesting, by the way, that Sigmund Freud developed his system of defense mechanisms at about the same time that Gurdjieff developed his concept of buffers.)

The buffers characteristically veil our negative character traits by reducing our inner friction through rationalizations, distortions, etc., and allowing us to live our mistakes unconsciously. But inner friction is absolutely necessary for the Work, in Gurdjieff's sense. The Enneagram shows clearly the nine strategies with which people fool themselves, living out their false personality types mechanically and completely unconsciously.

The idea of defense mechanisms was new at the beginning of the 20th century, and it was rejected strongly. Gurdjieff (this is what many American psychologists assume) did withhold it from his students. Nevertheless, from Gurdjieff's practical work, we can see that he used a method that demonstrated clearly to him the main weaknesses of his students. In order to make them realize this main weakness or false personality, on which the nine Enneagram types are based, Gurdjieff mercilessly exposed his students' weaknesses. During the notorious "toasts to the idiots," he put them under the influence of alcohol so that they would reveal themselves, and he always used to give them those tasks for which they were the least suited.

Whether or not Gurdjieff had the personality types of the Enneagram in the back of his mind during his work is hard to determine. In any case, he was coming from the basic Enneagram concept that each person has certain main characteristics that he does not see, but which are obvious to others.

When Ichazo worked out his concept of personality types in the Arica School, most of his co-workers knew Gurdjieff's work. Whether they skillfully worked Gurdjieff's viewpoints into their Enneagram, or whether Gurdjieff really was using an Enneagram of the nine types, cannot be determined—but it is insignificant. What is important is seeing that despite all the differences between Gurdjieff's work and Ichazo's types, there are points of contact between both systems (this, by the way, is obstinately denied by most of Gurdjieff's students).

My experience in my Gurdjieff group clearly shows that there are two ways to use the Enneagram in the Work:

1. The teacher uses the Enneagram of the

The Traditions of the Enneagram

Gurdjieff Tradition	Naranjo Tradition
Symbolic Forerunners • Achaldan Society (Atlantis) • Sarmoun Brotherhood (Babylon about 2,500 years before Christ)	• mysterious Sufi teacher (Afghanistan, beginning of the 20th century) • Gurdjieff's teaching • Arica Institute from 1970 on in Chile, from 1971 on in the U.S. • Esalen from the beginning of the '70s in California through Claudio Naranjo
Historical Forerunners • Sufi order of the Naqshbandi (from about the 15th or 16th century on) • Sufis in Buchara and the Near and Middle East at the end of the 19th century.	
George Ivanovitch Gurdjieff • First historical mention of the Enneagram, supported by documentary evidence, in Gurdjieff's Petersburg study group in 1916.	**Ecclesiastical Path** • Father Robert Ochs SJ (Jesuit Loyola University, Chicago) • Richard Riso (Jesuit, with an orientation toward psychoanalysis) who uses the terminology of Freud and Jung when referring to the Enneagram. • Richard Rohr • Andreas Ebert
Gurdjieff Students Who Spread the Enneagram • Peter Demian Ouspensky (1950) • John Godolphin Bennett (1974) • Ivan B. Popoff (1978) • Anthony G. E. Blake (1993) • Klausbernd Vollmar (1993)	**Way of Humanistic Psychology** • Eli Jaxon-Bear • Helen Palmer • Margaret Frings Keyes

types in order to make clear to his student the dark spot—the false personality. My teacher, at least, who does not know Ichazo's types, does that continually.

2. The Enneagram is used in order to clarify the consciousness processes. This use of the Enneagram is still completely in the hands of the Gurdjieffian teacher—the teacher of the Fourth Way.

3. The Enneagram as a System

"The Enneagram is not something that you can understand passively. You have to struggle with it, as Jacob could have struggled with the angel." —Anthony G. E. Blake

The Meaning of Classifications and Typologies

Typology as a Model of Understanding

Typologies represent an abstraction of the human being. They are created in order to see through the confusing diversity of human and other characteristic features—to view the important patterns. These patterns, as the typologies represent them, are helpful in gaining psychological knowledge and understanding. The goal of a typology like the one of the Enneagram is to create a clear differentiation among individual types of people and show how to recognize them more precisely. Typologies represent a kind of map that is projected onto human life so that we will be better able to orient ourselves.

Gurdjieff and Ichazo agree with the fact that the Enneagram is an image of the laws of psychic procedures in the human being. But the two pioneers of the Enneagram differ in how they estimate the consistency of human behavior.

For Gurdjieff, human behavior is hardly consistent—whether over a short period of time or in different situations. Different personality parts, or "I's," as Gurdjieff called them, dominate the human being, depending on the situation.

It is the central teaching of Gurdjieff that the uniform and constant "I" is illusionary. Instead, people have an accumulation of relatively chaotic, disorderly "I's." But, since we identify ourselves with the illusion of one "I," we fool ourselves and do not live our real selves. We think we have to represent something in the outer world, and we are dependent on our image instead of on our inner character. This makes us unhappy and limits our development.

Watch yourself for one day without trying to change yourself. You will notice how dependent you are on different outside impulses. You change your feelings and thus your mood several times a day. You were just friendly and patient, and immediately afterwards you react aggressively, coarsely, and stressed.

Based on such observations, Gurdjieff questioned the basic assumption of the typologies: that there is a relatively uniform "I." He was more in agreement with Johann Wolfgang von Goethe, who had Faust lament that two souls were living in his chest. According to Gurdjieff and Ouspensky, many more "souls" are bustling around in there!

For the philosophical reader, it is interesting to mention here that Gurdjieff, in his rejection of an unchangeable personality, is in the illustrious company of Buddha and of the British philosopher David Hume (1711–1776). Buddha considered the life of the human being as a process in which the human being changes himself permanently. For Buddha there is no Ego and no changeable personality. About 2,500 years later, David Hume denied, on the basis of his analyses of the human consciousness, that the human has a stable basic personality. For him, the human being is in the grip of different personalities, which come and go like mood shifts. This sentence could just as well have come from Gurdjieff.

Ichazo and the Christian tradition of the Enneagram, on the other hand, come from the idea that human behavior and personal attitudes are relatively constant in different situations and over longer periods of time. You can observe this in yourself if you have kept a diary. Read in your diary what moved you one or two years ago, and you may be startled at how little you have changed. We often have illusions about our capacity for change.

Both opinions may be correct. Gurdjieff's opinion of the inconsistent, fickle personality of the human being leads to schooling that produces more strength of consciousness, awakeness, and will in the individual. Ichazo's opinion of the relatively consistent stable personality, on the other hand, leads to a study of psychological personality types.

Such teachings of types have always existed. The best known and one of the oldest ones stems from the Greek doctor Hippocrates (about 460–377 B.C.), who distinguished the four temperaments—sanguine, phlegmatic, choleric, and melancholic—according to the predominance of the body fluids in the person. Galen (about 200–130 B.C.), the last great theorist of Greek antiquity, developed these classifications further.

Overall, classifications into fours were very popular in typologies, because "four" can be traced back to the archetypes of the four elements.

A more modern classification into fours stems from the Swiss psychologist Carl Gustav Jung, who divided human beings into four basic functions of the psyche that seem to determine his reactions:

- the thinking type, who strives to master the world intellectually

- the feeling type, who encounters the world with a spontaneous expression of feelings

- the perceptive type, who is determined by sensual awareness

- the instinctive type, who comprehends the world with intuition. That means by listening to an inner voice or to transcendental forces.

Jung, though, expands the original pattern of fours by distinguishing two basic poles:

- introverted (retreating into oneself)

- extroverted (directed toward the outside world).

Thus, according to Jung's type classification, eight different types come about, since each basic function of the psyche expresses itself either as introverted or extroverted. That means that Jung's types do not coincide with the Enneagram—which is based on nine types—without a certain amount of twisting and turning.

One of the best known teachings of types of modern times stems from Jung's forerunner Sigmund Freud (1856–1939), who distinguished four different types according to the phases of sexual development:[5]

- the oral type, who seeks to satisfy his lust through the mouth

- the anal type, who seeks to satisfy his lust through the anus

- the phallic type, who seeks to satisfy his lust through masturbation

- the genital type, who seeks to satisfy his lust through mature sexuality.

We can, if necessary, refer the three first types of this model to the Enneagram. The first third of the Enneagram would correspond to the oral phase, the second third to the anal, and the last third to the phallic phase.

* * *

With the teaching of types of the Enneagram, a classification into Nines lies before us, which, for ecclesiastical users of this pattern, represents the nine root sins of the human being:

- anger

- pride

- deceit

- envy (and ill will)

- greed

- fear

- gluttony

- lust

- sloth

At first glance, such an extensive model does not seem to have been chosen very wisely. By increasing the number of categories, the model, which was actually supposed to be unified, becomes more difficult to survey. On the other hand, such a typology certainly has the advantage of being relatively differentiated and not too abstract. Sometimes, the problem is that too few people fall concretely into the category of one type, and therefore each person has to be considered a mixed type.

According to my experience, many people fall into one of the nine categories of the Enneagram, but taking a more precise, differentiated look, they do display the tendency to mix with another type. It depends on how closely you look. The nine pure types offer a clear, distinct differentiation. Everyone can be allocated to one of the types without cheating. But if our interest is directed more toward the individual, we tend to see mixed types.

During the work of the Enneagram, we have to keep in mind that typologies represent subjective classifications of the human reality. Furthermore, we need to be aware not to lapse into pigeon-hole thinking. We tend

to label people who are more distant or foreign to us, and to quickly classify them in a type. We see people who are more familiar to us—and ourselves—much more as individuals, and we count them as mixed types.

If you want to distinguish types of human beings clearly, turn to Chapter 5 about the individual points of the Enneagram. If you want to comprehend the personality of someone in a more individual way, then read Chapter 6 about the dynamics of the model, where the combinations of the individual Enneagram types are discussed.

It is important to point out that different authors disagree considerably in the type classifications of the Enneagram. Richard Riso, for example, forces Freud's and Jung's categories into the Enneagram, without consideration of their connection, and at the same time attacks the differentiated work of Helen Palmer as being confusing, lacking, and incorrect. I, on the other hand, deviate in my concept of types[6] from that of Riso and Rohr/Ebert, since, according to Gurdjieff, the types are based on the basic classification of body (material), soul (emotion) and spirit (intellect). Eli Jaxon-Bear and Margaret Frings Keyes are essentially closer to me than is Riso's scurrilous mixture of scientific psychology with the Enneagram.

The Types of the Enneagram as Psychic Programs

The Enneagram represents a symbol of the programs that determine our lives. These programs are formed early in childhood and define our life strategies. The basic content of these programs is how we try to come to love and how we avoid suffering. The strategies determined in them lead to the shadow formation—a splitting off of the "evil and bad" parts of us. We learn to suppress those thoughts and feelings, so they gather themselves into a personal shadow that is far from consciousness.

Definition of the Shadow

The human being has a "shadow side, which by no means consists only of small weaknesses and blemishes, but of downright demonic dynamics.... To combine oneself with this shadow means saying yes to one's [carnal] instinct...."[7]

"The evil is always the other one, never ourselves," a human strategy says. Through it, we do not see reality as it is but as it should be ideally. That means our view of persons, situations, and things is distorted, and it takes a lot of energy to maintain this view.

If you examine your shadow side—for instance, what is embarrassing to you—without judgment, you will realize that through this acceptance an unexpected energy will flow through you. That is the energy that you tie up in suppressing your strategies, in order not to show your shadow. When we can look at our shadow, then, according to Jung, the self appears, which determines our uniform personality.

According to psychologist Margaret Frings Keyes, whose orientation is transactional analysis, the following strategies are consolidated into life-programs. They could be sketched out like this:

Enneagram type 1: Perfection
  Shadow: Rage

Enneagram type 2: Readiness to help
  Shadow: Manipulation

Enneagram type 3: Achievement
  Shadow: Rage for recognition (image)

Enneagram type 4: Extraordinariness
  Shadow: Sentimentality (moods)

Enneagram type 5: Knowledge
  Shadow: Retreat

Enneagram type 6: Security/safety
  Shadow: Fear and doubt

Enneagram type 7: Optimism
  Shadow: Nervous activity

Enneagram type 8: Fairness
  Shadow: Arrogance

Enneagram type 9: Peaceableness
  Shadow: Laziness

If we look at these programs objectively and come to understand our shadow, then we take off the clouded glasses that show us only a distorted reality and experience ourselves and our environment consciously. We will probably not behave differently—at least for the time being—but through this quality of the consciousness, the old way of behavior will become something fundamentally different.

Furthermore, the nine points of the Enneagram also contain our projections onto the outer and inner world.

Definition of Projection

"Projection means the transfer of a subjective procedure into an object... [They are] embarrassing, incompatible contents, which the subject gets rid of through projection as well as positive values, which are inaccessible to the subject for any kind of reason—for example, due to self-underestimation." —Carl G. Jung

These projections have the same effect as perception programs. The worst part of dealing with our projections is that we firmly believe in them. When we realize what we are projecting, through consciousness work with the Enneagram, we will succeed, as we do in the dissolution of the projected shadow, in seeing reality as it is. No projected image will stand between us and reality. Thus we will understand the world and others, because we understand our own projections. The Enneagram reveals all the fundamental projections of human beings, though it does not express them graphically.

In order to further understand one's own projections, Gurdjieff offers the consciousness exercise of self-remembering, which is allocated to the third Enneagram point. This self-remembering represents a schooling of the attention, which is necessary in order to develop one's own consciousness further. Referred to the Enneagram, this means that self-remembering is the pre-condition for continuing to step to the left side of the Enneagram.

EXERCISE: Self-Remembering

"When the yellow emperor woke up, he was very happy that he had found himself."
—Lao-Tzu

In the morning, after you get up, sit in a chair for about five minutes and close your eyes. Keep your spine as straight as possible. This holding the spine straight reminds you constantly of the required consciousness or awakeness.

Now try to sense your hands, your belly, your heart, and your head as distinctly as possible. Relax your face, especially, because with a relaxed face you will relax your entire body. At the same time, breathe in deeply and regularly.

Now you are completely calm.

If you want to intensify this exercise, concentrate on a spot a little less than an inch (2cm) above your navel. As you breathe, be conscious of how your breath is being pulled in through your nose, how it fills your lungs, and how it streams out at the designated spot above your navel. When you breathe in this way, you enhance your grounding.

While in this conscious relaxation, make up your mind to feel as conscious as possible two or three times at certain periods during the day, and to experience whatever situations you find yourself in as consciously as possible. Just be conscious of yourself and of the situation, without wanting to change it.

You could, for example, either choose points of time, such as three o'clock and five o'clock and so on, or in the morning during breakfast when you chew your first bite of food, during work and/or in the evening while reading, or during sunset.

At first you won't succeed at all in producing the required consciousness. It is important to keep trying, nevertheless, and let yourself be motivated by the realization of just how unconscious you are. As you continue to practice the exercise, you will most of the time remember to be conscious *after* the fixed point in time, and you will be shocked that

again an opportunity has escaped you. Don't get impatient; after a while you will succeed more and more. The more often you succeed, the greater the probability that consciousness will appear more often and easily at the desired point in time.

When you catch yourself once again being unconscious and lost in your thoughts, then it is important not to be disappointed and angry about it. Also, just as important is that when you succeed in keeping up your full consciousness in a situation, you do not give yourself a reward by telling yourself, "You really did that well!" We need to learn, in this exercise, to recognize how we are doing without evaluating it. If we cannot be conscious now and then and remind ourselves of our self, then this is a fact—no more or less—and we have recognized ourselves as we are. When we leave this factual level, we run the risk of identifying ourselves with the experiences of success and failure, and thus becoming dependent on outside evaluation.

If you succeed in being fully conscious at least once in a while, then you can try to do it in conflict situations (especially) in which you normally react negatively. If you succeed, you will realize that you are not identifying any more with your own feelings. Even though you are conscious of these feelings, you do not feel pushed to have to express them. Through this method, a lot of energy flows to you, which you can use to build up even more consciousness and eventually change your personality.

In this kind of self-observation, you retreat into yourself. Your attention is not directed towards the outside world, which robs you constantly of energy. Thus, you may have a chance to take back your projections. According to Gurdjieff, your environment lives on your projections.

Furthermore, you can apply this exercise very well in situations in which you fool yourself. To do that, first you need to observe which situations those are—observe them without wanting to change them—and then you need to try to stay as conscious as possible in these situations. Through this technique, you will automatically stop reacting mechanically. In that way, with patience and discipline, you can change all mechanical (unconscious) reactions, and especially projections.

An important effect of this consciousness exercise is that you will no longer identify yourself completely with the outside world, and you won't be dependent on it. You will, for example, regard your work as a game that you strive to play well. If, in addition to this exercise, you go over the past day once every evening before falling asleep, or if you keep a diary regularly, that will help as well to strengthen your consciousness. You will realize clearly how little consciousness you usually produce in your everyday life. That is an important insight, whose energy you can use to produce a higher force of consciousness.

If, finally, you have come so far that you determine that throughout the past day you were conscious of yourself frequently, then you need to make up your mind to achieve a larger amount of consciousness on the following day.

It is another aspect of this consciousness exercise that shows us how much we are dependent on the outside world, and that we actually do not own a consistent Ego (or willpower or discipline). Through this exercise, we can achieve a relatively consistent Ego.

Commentary

I want to mention a modern Buddhist story that not only illustrates the parallels between the Gurdjieff Work and Buddhist methods, but also graphically demonstrates the secret of self-remembering.

A modern master incited his monks by promising them that the person who could live seven days consciously would be enlightened.

One young monk immediately began with this exercise and realized after five minutes that his attention had failed and his thoughts were wandering about uncontrollably. So, he began anew, only to realize again that he had forgotten and lost his attention after some minutes.

At the end of seven days, he was not enlightened, but he was aware how often he fled into the world of fantasy and how weak he really was, since he kept up his attention for only a few minutes at the most. Now he could really begin to work at his enlightenment successfully.

Self-remembering is similar, closely observed, to a meditation exercise. It helps us, through the remembrance of ourselves, and through becoming conscious of our body, to become completely calm. This deep calm is, according to Gurdjieff, required so that we can make contact with our higher feeling—and thinking—centers. Normally, we have contact only with our lower feeling—and thinking—centers. The higher centers lie on the level of the intuition and can only have an effect when we are completely empty—when we do not identify ourselves with our thoughts and emotions, but merely perceive them without wanting to change them.

Unfortunately, we often tend to expect too much in such basic consciousness exercises. We think that after some exercise, the big enlightenment will come upon us like a dramatic event. That is not the case—I have to disappoint you in this respect—nothing dramatic happens. You will sense yourself intensively and become inwardly as well as externally completely calm. In order to reach this state, it helps to concentrate on your body or on one body-part and not to expect anything.

This elementary attention exercise will help you get to know yourself on many levels. Without such an observation technique, you will be inclined to concentrate only on "thinking" and will not be able to perceive more complex impressions at all.

The first and most basic teaching of Buddha says, "Don't get attached!"—which means taking the attitude of non-identification with your feelings and fantasies. The goal of this exercise is the same. Since Gurdjieff lived for some time in Tibet and met Lamas there who were in on the secret, the closeness between the consciousness work in Tibetan Buddhism and the schools of the Fourth Way is not surprising.

This exercise of self-remembering can also be examined through the Enneagram:

1. You are conscious of the fact that you have to change something, which corresponds to the first Enneagram point.

2. You inform yourself about how you can change yourself, which corresponds to the second Enneagram point.

3. You come to the exercise of self-remembering at the third Enneagram point.

4. The exercise of self-remembering causes more difficulties than expected. You realize that you are almost never conscious of yourself, which annoys you at the fourth Enneagram point.

5. The difficulties of doing this exercise remain, but it becomes clear at the fifth Enneagram point what this consciousness exercise boils down to. The frustration in this exercise is used to build up greater motivation for doing consciousness work in your daily life.

6. At the sixth Enneagram point, you meet a person who shows you how to progress with this exercise. (It could also be a book.)

7. At the seventh Enneagram point you succeed in moving consciously and attentively through life.

8. At the eighth Enneagram point you have reached your goal—to dedicate yourself fully to consciousness work.

The monk in the Buddhist story on page 20 went through exactly the same steps.

The Enneagram as Symbol

"Neither the head nor the heart alone can lead the searching person further... Work with a symbol requires simultaneous endeavors of head and heart." —Boris Mouravieff

In classical Greece a word or a sign was understood by the term *Symbolon*. With its help, those who were initiated into the mysteries of Ceres, Cybele, and Mithras could recognize each other. You can also consider the Enneagram as such a Symbolon. Gurdjieff students used it to identify each other until recently. But since the 1980s, when the Enneagram was popularized by the Ichazo school, it has largely lost this function.

According to Carl Gustav Jung, a symbol is an energy transformer—a psychic happening. You could also say that a symbol is the graphic expression of an idea. At the same time, something mysterious is also part of its nature. It is never completely comprehensible, and it always contains more than you can recognize at first sight. A symbol clarifies something unknown and requires a certain amount of inner participation from the observer.

The Enneagram as a symbol represents the idea of the universe as well as forms of appearance of the human psyche. It is basically—as Gurdjieff stressed again and again—only emotionally comprehensible. That's why Gurdjieff tried to convey the Enneagram through the Movements.

The Enneagram was originally thought of as a precise source of information for seekers of the truth. You can comprehend such a symbol as the Enneagram only through your two higher centers. Access to those centers, though, is only possible from the seventh Enneagram point onward. This is because the Enneagram conveys laws that lie beyond the world of the intellect, the five senses, and our emotions. We can think of the Enneagram as a map that shows us the path into an area beyond our daily consciousness. At the same time, the Enneagram illustrates something unknown and something that is hard to recognize—the dynamics of the human psyche as reflected in the nine types. It opens our eyes to a new perspective on the world and widens our visual angle.

One symbol serves, according to Jung, to encompass the whole human being. The recognition of the symbol transforms the person's psychic energy and opens his eyes completely. This reminds us of another cosmic symbol—the Mandala—as we know it from Tibetan Buddhism. You could see the Enneagram also as a special Mandala.

The Indian Mandala specialist Madhu Khanna writes:

> Above all, one believes of them [the Mandalas] that they make up the inner base of the forms and formations that are visible in the universe. Just as any kind of matter, however its outer structure may be conditioned, is made of a specific basic matter—the atom—so may every aspect of the world in its structural form be perceived as Yantra [a geometric Mandala].[8]

Both the Enneagram and the Mandala are cosmic diagrams that help you to meditate. They are symbols that will lead you to your own center. Both the Mandala and Enneagram guide our consciousness to the Self (or God). At least, they awaken an intuition of something superpersonal. The character of this superpersonal state—to which, in the last analysis, every symbol points—is never completely comprehensible. As Goethe said it: "The true, identical with the divine, never lets itself be recognized by us directly: we see it only in the symbol."

Truth-seekers always need a symbol, because the truth itself is not visible. Therefore, among the African Arabas, the Mandala is called "a pair of glasses" or "expansion." The Mandala as well as the Enneagram represent help in seeing, in order to look deeper and further at what is holding the world together. Like the Enneagram, the Mandala reflects the human spirit in its entirety and in its way of functioning. Both symbols reveal cosmic truths, and we regard them as diagrams that illustrate the spiritual aspects of divine truth. Thus, it is not surprising that in Gurdjieff's book, *Meetings with Remarkable Men*, a group of people who call themselves "truth-seekers" tracks down the symbol of the Enneagram.

EXERCISE: THE MANDALA

When we work with our feelings and thought forms through meditation, the first step to a higher consciousness is that we observe our inner images as objectively as possible. In this observation it is essential that we do not identify ourselves with these images, feelings, and thoughts. We win this distance in a second step, by letting geometric forms come about out of our inner images. These forms represent Mandalas. That means that each inner image can be transformed into a certain Mandala and take on an aesthetic form. I am of the opinion that this inner aesthetic represents a higher form of love.

EXERCISE: THE INNER IMAGES OF THE ENNEAGRAM

I recommend that you meditate with the Enneagram by making your inner images of it more specific. This exercise will help you to distance yourself from your feelings without thrusting them aside. That is what is meant by the "transformation of the feelings," which is spoken of by Tibetan Buddhists and teachers of the schools of the Fourth Way.

When you see the Mandala or the Enneagram clearly in front of your inner eye, concentrate on the image in such a way that you withdraw your energy from all other thoughts, images, and feelings. Thereby, you will notice a deep calm, coupled with a highly relaxed attention.

In the next step, try to slowly turn this visualized Enneagram, because no Mandala is rigid; all are in constant movement. Only that which moves and changes permanently expresses life.

You can let the Enneagram turn faster and faster, and then let it become smaller, until its essence is concentrated on a small dot in front of your inner eye. Hold this dot for five breaths and then slowly return to your everyday life.

Commentary

This meditation exercise is not so simple, and you will need to practice it over and over again. But you will realize that the visualization and movement of the Enneagram become easier and easier, and your impulse to "float away" and get distracted during the exercise, less and less strong.

In order to perform this meditation exercise as I have described it here, you will need at least half a year of regular exercise. Always keep in mind that mastering the exercise immediately is not the point, because the learning that comes from this exercise will convey to you essential things about the Enneagram and how you can use it.

You could notice during this meditation:

- The Enneagram is something alive that is always in movement.

- It is an energy transformer, which can be comprehended only emotionally.

- The understanding of the Enneagram changes us in such a way that we can use our energies for higher purposes.

The Enneagram symbolizes at the least:

- cosmic and psychological laws

- a personal path to self-development and a model that explains the courses that processes follow

- a system of individual reaction tendencies and points of view.

Since it organizes, among other things, the classification of human beings into nine types, we could ask whether these images are archetypal. In the sense of basic patterns of our perceptions, the answer would probably be yes. The Enneagram symbolizes nine basic patterns by which we perceive our inner and outer reality, and at the same time, it points at something higher—a cosmic reference. But since reality is more complex than the Enneagram, it is important to avoid one-sided thinking when using it.

A basic rule in the application of the Enneagram, as applied to personality types, should be that you need to apply the Enneagram to yourself, so that you become conscious of your own projections, before you apply it to others. Otherwise, you won't be using the Enneagram as a symbol that widens your awareness, but as a projection instrument, which restricts it.

What You Can Understand with the Enneagram

Processes of Growth

When we speak about the Enneagram, we usually think first of the personality types. But our own inner growth process can also be understood via the Enneagram. Work with the Enneagram enables you to see processes in a new connection. Your own growth process becomes clear, allowing you to perceive it in a new way.

When you realize that something in your life has gone wrong, you feel unhappy. Then you find a teacher, begin to work with consciousness exercises and thus, through your victory over inner resistances, you come closer to your goal—to being the person that you really are. Not only can you understand the course of this process through the Enneagram, but it can also show you the next step in your personal development. In this application of the Enneagram, according to the tradition of Gurdjieff, you would find that you, in the last analysis, contain in yourself all the Enneagram types, and that you can live the positive possibilities of all these types as a developed human being.

- At Enneagram Point 1, you will notice your dissatisfaction and that you will become unhappy if you live against your true "I." But this sense is present only indistinctly as a vague feeling. Since point 1 connects with point 7 and point 4, you get an idea about your goal (point 7), and you will assume that must change you emotionally (point 4).

- At Enneagram Point 2, you gather all kinds of information about what you can do in order to change. Through this process, the goal becomes clearer (since 2 connects with point 8) and, as at point 1, you fear the impending emotional changes (point 4).

- At Enneagram Point 3, a new quality comes into play, which affects us from the outside and helps us to really take on the path of change toward our true Self. The new quality might be a teacher, a book, or a psychotherapist. In the Gurdjieff tradition, this is where you begin to work with the consciousness exercises.

- At Enneagram Point 4, you move into the field of the emotions where Enneagram Point 5 also belongs. Here you suffer from the rigidity of your emotions and often flee back into the past (points 1 and 2). Under emotional pressure you frequently lose sight of your goal here. The consciousness exercises help you to remain in the growth process.

- At Enneagram Point 5, you begin to understand your emotions at least once in a while. You begin to perceive them,

but do not identify with them. Through this, you see your goal (points 7 and 8) very clearly and seizably close.

- At Enneagram Point 6, again a strong impulse must affect us from the outside, since otherwise our goal would seem to be unattainable. Here again a teacher, who can be a person, an external situation, or a friend, helps us to continue with patience and willpower.

- At Enneagram Point 7, we have finally reached at least the lower step of our goal.

- At Enneagram Point 8, we are capable of dedicating ourselves completely to our goal and of realizing ourselves.

- At Enneagram Point 9, we start the whole process over again on a higher level.

As an overview, that will do for now. In Chapter 5 about the individual points of the Enneagram, you can read in more detail about the different levels of this developmental process.

The Benefit of This Enneagram View

- In this view of the Enneagram, you recognize your personal developmental path.

- Through this recognition, you can get through hard times more easily, as the Enneagram Points 4 and 5 characterize them.

- You realize the necessity of having outside help (Points 3 and 6).

- You become conscious of the danger of turning unfruitfully in the circle—for example, turning back at Enneagram Point 4 to the old ways of behavior of points 1 and 2.

How Processes Follow a Principle

Studying the Enneagram, we can look at not only psychological processes, but ones that are social or economic—in short, all processes that are based on human action. The impetus for this concept came especially from Gurdjieff's student John Godolphin Bennett.

- Enneagram Points 1 and 2 describe the material basics of the process. The first Enneagram point examines the basic pre-conditions for the process. The second Enneagram point examines the consequences that result from these basic pre-conditions. On the economic level, these would be the means of production.

- Enneagram Point 3 introduces a new level, namely, the idea of where the process is to be steered to. Again, in the field of economics, we might be dealing with a production idea.

- Enneagram Points 4 and 5 occupy themselves with the material that has to be altered. At point 4, laborious work is usually required. At point 5, what is achieved has to be organized toward the goal.

- Again we go to a new level with Enneagram Point 6, where the outside world as market and consumer comes into play.

- Enneagram Points 7 and 8 show the result of the work. The goal of the process that you present to the outside world is evident at point 7. At point 8, the end-product of the work is sold to the consumer, in order then, at point 9, to start from the existing experiences and maybe begin a new, improved production series.

The Enneagram as an Aid in Understanding Your Personal Processes

Which Enneagram point corresponds to your personal processes?

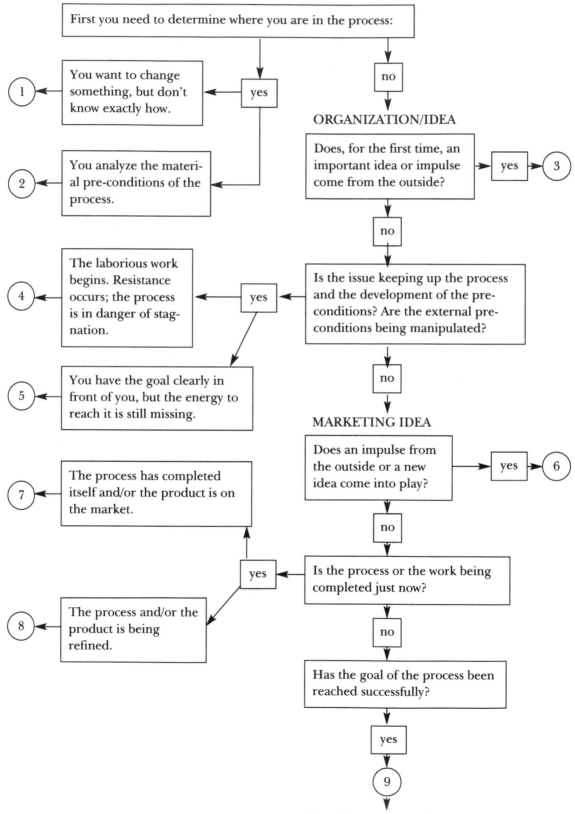

Transition to a new phase

26

The Enneagram as an Aid in Understanding Your Personal Processes

Which Enneagram point corresponds to my personal development?

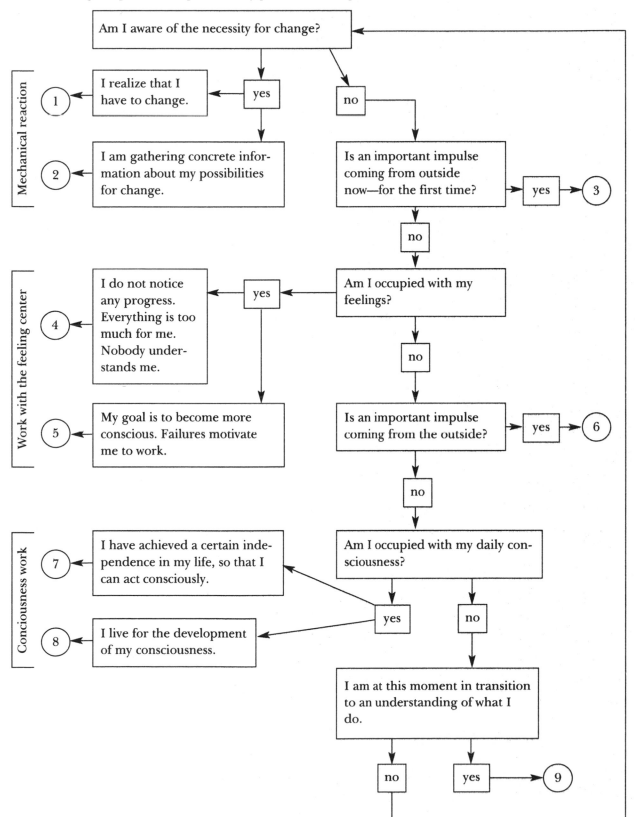

Benefit of this Enneagram View

It shows:

- the course of a process following a principle (points 1 to 9)
- what keeps up this process (points 3 and 6)
- where you will come upon difficulties (point 4 and partially 5).

From these steps, the best way to deal with the process becomes clear.

- It shows which level of a process has to be looked at, how the different levels of the process are connected, and what needs to be considered in what sequence.
- It shows where you need new impulses in a process (points 3 and 6), which are given through a change in level.

Basically, the Enneagram, in this application, helps you to:

- recognize a favorable opportunity

- seize this opportunity in its complexity

- predict the result of your choices

- set up a realistic plan.

In order to learn how to work with the Enneagram, it helps to analyze specific problems from everyday life using the Enneagram model. Try to figure out where you are in the process now and how you came to be there. Furthermore, you can see from this Enneagram point what the future course of your life could be.

You can understand the upcoming exercises better with the Enneagram. Let's look at two examples.

The Divorce

A client of mine tried to understand the separation from her husband via the Enneagram as follows:

- Enneagram Point 1: A vague dissatisfaction with the relationship makes her take a closer look at her situation.

- Enneagram Point 2: The dissatisfaction is easier to recognize in its consequences and partially also in its causes.

- Enneagram Point 3: She comes across a book that causes her to see a therapist. That is the outside impulse at the first shock point.

- Enneagram Point 4: On one hand, only now does the full extent of the emotional disaster become clear. On the other hand, doubts come up as to whether she should separate from him or whether she should work harder, after all, to save the relationship.

- Enneagram Point 5: It becomes clear to her that a separation is necessary, but the last push and concrete steps in the direction of a separation are still missing.

- Enneagram Point 6: The client finds a new apartment and a new job. That is the second external impulse, which brings her closer to her goal.

- Enneagram Point 7: The client gets a divorce.

- Enneagram Point 8: She frees herself emotionally from her former husband and begins to see new men.

- Enneagram Point 9: She begins a new life.

If you look at each of the individual Enneagram points, you can easily see the benefit of Enneagram work. The two lines that originate at each Enneagram point clarify the perspectives on the situation. For example, you can see at the first Enneagram point the preliminary goal—the divorce—at Enneagram Point 7, because one of the lines extends right to it. At the same time, the other line extends to

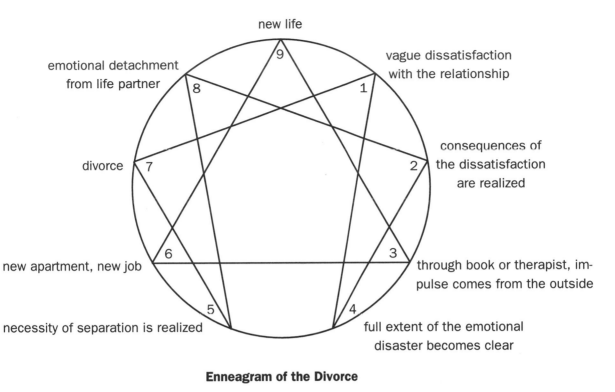

Enneagram of the Divorce

Point 4, whose keynote is emotion, and doubts appear, which characterize Enneagram Point 4.

At the second Enneagram point, you understand that, in the last analysis, it is necessary to have emotional detachment from the partner (Enneagram Point 8), and still certain doubts exist (Enneagram Point 4).

At the fourth Enneagram point, you need to be careful to keep the doubts from letting you fall back again into the old situation (Enneagram Points 1 and 2).

At Enneagram Point 5, your goal is clearly in front of you (Enneagram Points 7 and 8), but the last push is missing, which brings you to the sixth Enneagram point.

The seventh and eighth Enneagram points, on the one hand, give you a look into the future by pointing to the Enneagram Points 1 and/or 2, which belong to the new process. On the other hand, they point to the fifth Enneagram point, which brings the emotional clarity you need in order to see what has to be done.

With this method, all kinds of everyday problems can be treated.

Another brief example: I want to rebuild my house.

- Enneagram Point 1: I am dissatisfied with the space in my house.

- Enneagram Point 2: It becomes clear to me that it would be possible to get more space.

- Enneagram Point 3: I see the reconstruction of the house of an architect, which I like very much.

- Enneagram Point 4: I have doubts about whether I can afford the reconstruction, but I would like to create a comfortable home.

- Enneagram Point 5: I think about possible financing and consult with the architect.

- Enneagram Point 6: The architect brings his plans, which thrill me.

- Enneagram Point 7: Financing is secured. I will get the space that I was hoping for through the reconstruction.

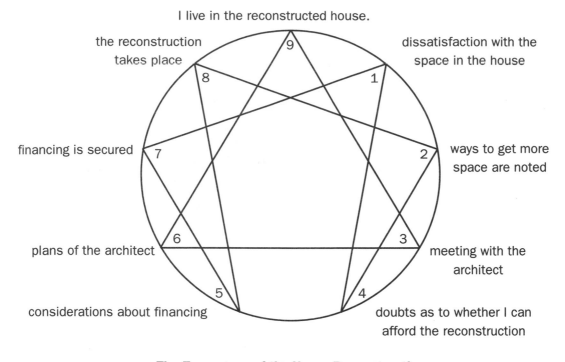

I live in the reconstructed house.

the reconstruction takes place

dissatisfaction with the space in the house

financing is secured

ways to get more space are noted

plans of the architect

meeting with the architect

considerations about financing

doubts as to whether I can afford the reconstruction

The Enneagram of the House Reconstruction

- Enneagram Point 8: The reconstruction takes place.

- Enneagram Point 9: I live in the reconstructed house.

Look for yourself at the connections between the individual points.

I think these two examples will show how you can use the Enneagram creatively in solving your own problems.

The Order of the Human Energy Centers—the Chakras

Definition of a Chakra

"Chakra," which means "circle" in Sanskrit, is the name for an energy center of the human body and partially also of the earth.

The seven chakras of the human body absorb energy, collect, and transform it. They mark the points at which the spiritual and the physical merge and penetrate each other.

There are seven main chakras:

- the root—or Muladhara chakra—at the lowest point of the spine

- the sacral—or Svadisthana chakra—at the genitals

- the solar plexus—or Manipura chakra (called "Hara" in Japan)—in the navel region

- the heart—or Anahata chakra—in the area of the heart

- the throat—or Vishuddha chakra—in the neck area

- the Third Eye or Ajna chakra—between the eyebrows

- the crown—or Sahasrara-chakra—thought to be partially at and partially above the vertex of the head.

The inner space of the Enneagram results in an irregular heptagon, in which the seven chakras can be arranged.

The root chakra is allocated to Enneagram Point 1; the sacral chakra to Enneagram Point 2; the throat chakra to Enneagram Point 7; the Third Eye to Enneagram Point 8; the crown chakra to Enneagram Point 9.

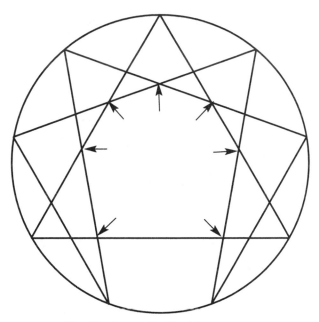

The Heptagon in the Enneagram

This allocation is easy to understand, since the individual chakras lie opposite the Enneagram points. The two centers of gravity (focal points) of the body—the solar plexus chakra (navel chakra) and the heart chakra—are allocated to Enneagram Points 3/4 and 5/6.

It's interesting that the connecting lines of the Enneagram show us the paths in the body through which energy streams—the way the individual chakras are connected with each other. From this, you can figure out how to proceed when one chakra is blocked. A blockage produces an energy imbalance in the chakras that are connected with it.

For Gurdjieff, the human body has three energy centers:

1. the center of the belly, which is where the navel—or Manipura chakra—is assumed to be.

2. the heart center, which is where the heart—or Anahata chakra—is assumed to be.

3. the head center, which is where the Third Eye—or the Ajna chakra—is assumed to be.

According to this allocation of human energy centers, the following division of the Enneagram comes about:

Enneagram Points 1 and 2—The Belly Center

This is the center that reacts fastest, also called the "movement center." It corresponds to the material structure of our body and is the so-called "instinct center," which reacts spontaneously to outside stimuli.

Enneagram Points 4 and 5—The Heart Center

This is the center that regulates our feelings and is therefore often called the "feeling center." It controls our relationships consciously and unconsciously.

Enneagram Points 7 and 8—The Head Center

This is the center that reacts slowest. It is connected with the intellect, as well as with the consciousness. According to Gurdjieff, thinking is closely connected with acting, since taking action needs conscious planning.

Each of these three centers is, according to Gurdjieff, connected with all the other centers and can also take over the functions of the other two. But if, for example, the intellectual center takes over the function of the feeling center, that leads inevitably to an inadequate conduct of life.

The Benefit of this Enneagram View
Illustration of the energy streams in the chakras
Practical therapy instruction for harmonizing the chakras

The Order of the Colors

The order of the colors in the Enneagram is arranged according to primary and secondary colors. And it is in this example that the dynamic structure of the Enneagram shows itself most clearly, because two sensible allocations are possible.

1. The primary colors are arranged at the triangle points in the Enneagram:

Blue at Enneagram Point 3

Yellow at Enneagram Point 6

Red at Enneagram Point 9

The secondary colors are arranged at the following Enneagram points:

Green at the Enneagram Points 4 and 5

Orange at the Enneagram Points 7 and 8

Violet at the Enneagram Points 1 and 2.

The cold colors stand on the right side of the Enneagram, the warm ones on the left. Red stands at the top. The polarity of the colors between light and darkness is symbolized by the axis of the Enneagram Points 3 (blue—in terms of color, the representative of darkness) and 6 (yellow, in terms of color, representative of the light).

2. The order of the colors according to the perspectives in the Enneagram:

Red: Enneagram Points 1 and 9

Violet: Enneagram Point 2

Blue: Enneagram Points 3 and 4

Green: Enneagram Point 5

Yellow: Enneagram Point 6

Orange: Enneagram Points 7 and 8

Enneagram Point 1 connects all the primary colors, Enneagram Point 8 all the secondary colors. From the Enneagram Points 2 and 7 come the complementary colors—blue-orange and green-red.

The Benefit of this Enneagram View

The principles of the six colors can be seen graphically in many ways in the Enneagram.

1. Primary and secondary colors

2. Cold and warm colors

3. Colors of light and darkness

4. Complementary colors

Cosmic Connections

Astronomy

The planets also arrange themselves in a natural way in the Enneagram, according to the laws of their movement and the distance of their orbits from the sun.

- Mercury, as the one next to the sun and as the fastest planet, is at Enneagram Point 1 (octave[9] Uranus on point 7).

- Venus is the planet following Mercury at Enneagram Point 2 (octave Neptune on point 8). Like Mercury, it shows a periodic succession as morning and evening star.

- Earth and moon as the "heart of the universe" (Gurdjieff) are at Enneagram Point 3. According to Gurdjieff, with the third Enneagram point, we enter the area of feeling. It is probably no coincidence that there was an erratic increase in psychological literature when, at the end of the sixties, the first human being landed on the moon.

Now the planets that follow are visible periodically:

- Mars, with its complex orbit at Enneagram Point 4, corresponding to the feelings

- the Asteroid belt at the gap and/or at the lower center of the Enneagram (so-called Points 4 and 5)

- Jupiter in the center between sun and Pluto (orbit at Enneagram Point 5).

- Saturn as the last planet to be seen with the naked eye at Enneagram Point 6.

In the last third, the other planets follow:

- Uranus at Enneagram Point 7

- Neptune at Enneagram Point 8

- Pluto at Enneagram Point 9.

When Uranus was discovered at the end of the 18th century, it was a time of declarations (1776 in the United States, 1789 in France), that stressed the rights of the individual. At the same time, Franz Anton Mesmer (1734–1815), one of the forerunners of Sigmund Freud, triggered a mass movement that focused on the psyche of the individual. With Uranus at Enneagram Point 7, individuality was born. That coincides precisely with Gurdjieff's conception of the Enneagram—namely, that at Enneagram Point 7, the human being, for perhaps the first time, would be viewed as a responsible individual with free will.

The Enneagram and Astronomy

Order of the planets according to the distance of their orbits from the sun (Enneagram Points 1 to 9)

The change of morning and evening star (Enneagram Points 1 and 2)

Planets of comparable visibility deviation (points 4 and 5)

All outer (superpersonal) planets that cannot be seen without technical assistance in the last third of the Enneagram.

Astrology

In astrology, the human psyche is projected toward the sky. You can also refer to the Enneagram as a key to the human psyche and astrology.

The Order of the Planets

1. Personal planets

Mercury occupies Enneagram Point 1.

Venus stands at Enneagram Point 2.

Earth and Moon are in the shock point (Enneagram Point 3).

Mars is at Enneagram Point 4.

Jupiter is at Enneagram Point 5.

Saturn, as "guard of the threshold" at the transition to the invisible, stands at the second shock point, Enneagram Point 6.

2. Superpersonal planets

In the last third of the Enneagram, the outer planets follow:

Uranus at Enneagram Point 7 (octave of point 1, Mercury)

Neptune at Enneagram Point 8 (octave of point 2, Venus)

Pluto at Enneagram Point 9 (octave of point 4, Mars)

Order of the Zodiacal Signs

The order of the constellations is also reflected in the Enneagram:

Taurus at Enneagram Point 1

Cancer at Enneagram Point 2

Leo at Enneagram Point 3

Virgo at Enneagram Point 4

Scorpio at Enneagram Point 5

Sagittarius at Enneagram Point 6

Capricorn at Enneagram Point 7

Pisces at Enneagram Point 8

Aries at Enneagram Point 9 (which can also be seen as the beginning of the Enneagram—Enneagram Point 0).

The three fire signs—Aries, Leo, and Sagittarius—stand at the corners of the so-called "divine triangle" of the Enneagram. When we stand at Enneagram Point 1, we see all three earth signs. From Enneagram Point 8, we see all the fire signs. No Enneagram point corresponds to the three air signs—Gemini, Libra, and Aquarius.

The reason for this is, on one hand, that a system of nines cannot without a break depict a system of twelves. On the other hand, we could also argue that air energy, symbolizing the intellectual, is so overemphasized in our society that it does not have to be prominent in the Enneagram as well.

The Benefit of this Enneagram View

- It shows the law of the octaves: Mercury (1)/Uranus (7), Venus (2)/Neptune (8), and Mars (4)/Pluto (9).

- The planets are divided into personal and superpersonal planets. The personal planets are all in the first points of the Enneagram; the superpersonal ones in the last points.

- Earth/Moon as the "heart of our solar system," and Pluto, as the representative of the Sun, stand at 3, 6, and 9, the shock points of the Enneagram.

- the signs of the zodiac are arranged according to the elements: Fire signs on the triangle (3, 6, 9); earth signs are seen from point 1 (1, 4, 7); and the water signs are seen from point 8 (8, 2, 5). Air signs are not represented.

How Do You Find Your Enneagram Point?

At the beginning, it has to be emphasized that you basically combine all the Enneagram types in yourself. It happens—to me as to others—that most of the time, when doing the different Enneagram tests,[10] I correspond to two or even three types. Especially in different situations, we can recognize different types in ourselves.

While we all usually seem to show, quite mechanically, the reactions of one type or of a type combination, especially when in need or in danger, I have noticed again and again that the same person in different situations may react like different Enneagram types.

Why does this happen? Unity of consciousness is an illusion. The "I" of the human being changes at the same speed as his thoughts and feelings. In reality, the human being is always another person.

Luckily, most of us have not become so inflexible that we have the behavior spectrum of only one type. For that reason alone, I think of Enneagram tests as being more a fun evening's entertainment than an instrument that provides scientifically valid and significant statements. The whole idea of psychological tests, whose world is restricted to measurement and numbers, seems to me to contradict everything the Enneagram stands for. Intuition should be in the forefront in dealing with such a symbol. An Enneagram that is reduced to a scientific model can no longer be one that challenges us to creativity and self-recognition. It would decay into a kind of intelligence test in which you wouldn't know what you were measuring. This workbook will not concern itself with this "castrated" Enneagram. I want to describe a lively one. But I have to admit that I myself designed an Enneagram test (PET—Practical Enneagram Test) that was published in my introductory book, *The Enneagram.* But that test is not characterized by scientific claims of significant values and high validity. It is rather a matter of getting to know the Enneagram better through an exploration of some questions and getting to know yourself better as well. The primary goal is not really to recognize your type, but to get an idea of where you stand in your life and what you need to do, according to the teachings of the Enneagram. But since, despite all reservations, everybody is still curious about which Enneagram type he is, I want to give you the stimulus that will help you find out. My test may not work as fast as those in some magazines, but it will assist you to see yourself more realistically and to understand and use the Enneagram creatively for your self-awareness.

If you are in a special hurry, you can find your Enneagram type by answering the key questions at the end of the description of each type (in Chapter 5, "The Individual Points of the Enneagram").

The advantage of the typology in this book lies in the fact that the individual types are not set off sharply against each other. Don Richard Riso and Markus Becker try, in their teachings of types, to show the Enneagram as a technical instrument that corresponds to scientific theory. In the schools of the Fourth Way, on the other hand, we try to keep the human being in sight in all his inner and outer reality—not as a statistic—and thus to get to creative statements. I am concerned with real knowledge and insight that can be used practically—not a sterile university science course.

EXERCISE: Finding the Enneagram Type Through Consciousness

Much better than taking an Enneagram test is the following consciousness exercise, which makes clear in which situations you are inclined toward which Enneagram type and, at the same time, on which developmental stage of the Enneagram you stand. First, become aware of specific recurring reactions and then look them up in the listings of the individual points of the Enneagram. If you want to know where you stand in your personal development, you can refer to the types to see how they correspond to a certain kind of reaction or process. You can also proceed the other way around, by reading the passages about the nine Enneagram types and about the nine consciousness stages of the Enneagram. Then figure out which description fits you best and which you reject the most. The description that, in your opinion, fits you best will, most of the time, reflect your type pretty well, since in the last analysis, nobody knows you better than yourself. The type that you reject is connected with your shadow and

probably represents at least a part of it. If the statements of two types apply to you, then look up the mixed type among the combinations of the individual types, and let these descriptions affect you.

EXERCISE: Finding the Enneagram Type with the Help of a Diary

Besides self-remembering (page 19), regular journaling can help you to recognize your Enneagram type, as well as your developmental stage. If you have been keeping a diary for some time, then re-read the last entries and try to characterize your behavior and your mental attitude as precisely as possible in one or two sentences.

Another way is to write three things into your diary that you like to do, and then three things that you very much dislike doing.

After that, note briefly what you like so much about the first three things, and what you cannot stand about the other three things. Then look in the list of the descriptions of the Enneagram types for the one that best fits these likes and dislikes.

What often helps me to see clearly the pattern I'm reacting to at the moment is to observe the contents of my mind. I proceed as follows:

I go into a meditative state, my diary lying next to me. As thoughts arise, I write them down immediately. After the meditation, I look at these notes and try to characterize them as briefly and precisely as possible. Then I look up the mental attitude in the listing of the individual Enneagram points.

These exercises point up the limitations of the Enneagram model, because, even though it presents the types astonishingly well, you will also find situations in which no Enneagram type seems to apply. After all, a model is only a model...

4. The Structure of the Enneagram

"What is God? He is length,
height, and depth."
—Bernhard von Clairvaux

At first, the Enneagram faces us as a geometric structure. We can presuppose a geometric consciousness in all living beings, because every form of life produces certain geometric growth forms. In the schools of the Fourth Way, we assume that geometric consciousness has its effect in the intellectual part of the movement center. For this reason—in order to come closer to the Enneagram—I think it is important to draw Enneagrams freehand every day for a few minutes.

As you see, the Enneagram is in a strange way both symmetrical and asymmetrical. The right and the left side of the Enneagram are mirror images of each other. The upper and lower part of the Enneagram, on the other hand, are constructed differently. Therefore, the Enneagram fascinates us through a very special geometry.

Geometric forms make up our world, reflecting the rhythms and vibrations from which it is built. All our senses react to geometric impulses: We smell, for example, the pleasant aroma of a flower, because geometrically arranged molecules affect our smell-receptors. Also sight, like all our other senses, is dependent on the geometry of the impulses that affect the sense organs. The entire outside world, as a world of matter, is based on geometric forms, which, in the last analysis, can be traced back to the archetypal circle, triangle, and square. So it is not surprising that the Enneagram as a geometric structure symbolizes the structure or the rhythm of nature.

The Construction of the Enneagram

The Enneagram is constructed from:

1. a circle
2. an equilateral triangle
3. an irregular hexagon

The two basic geometric forms are the circle and triangle—and then there is a special form of the hexagon

The Individual Lines

THE CIRCLE

The circle symbolizes the world, in which everything takes place.

We speak of the globe as a circle. Medieval mystics saw the world soul as a circle. The circle symbolizes eternal recurrence, and furthermore, it is an archetypal symbol of the soul and of the feminine.

As we have seen, the Sanskrit word for circle is "Mandala," which describes the circle as a geometric figure, as well as the movements and processes that live in the circle.

Witches claim that they broaden their everyday consciousness through the circle. So, let's begin our exercise with the empty circle, fill it with the lines of the Enneagram, and trace the movements and processes that broaden our everyday consciousness.

EXERCISE: The Circle

This exercise is based on the fact that you can only understand a diagram like the Enneagram correctly when you have constructed it yourself with a compass and a ruler.

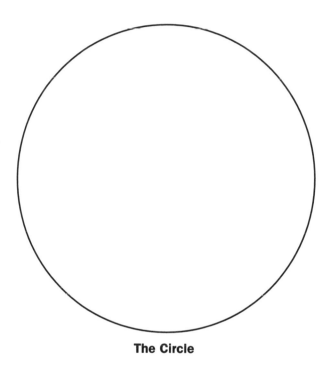

The Circle

Start by making any kind of a circle with the compass, and meditate with it before you. This is the circle that describes the world, in which all the processes and the development of the human being take place. Within this circle we find all types of human beings and all the happenings of our world. In it everything takes place that you can explain with the Enneagram. This circle, though, still corresponds to the empty world of the creation. It is the womb out of which our world is being born.

The circle, in its current form, corresponds to the number zero (0). That is the number from which all other numbers emerge. This is shown graphically in Arabic, where the word "Sifr" means "zero" as well as "number." While all other numbers are thought of as representing certain elements, the number zero is based on the idea of a beginning that is not comprehensible to us.

THE TRIANGLE

With the next step, the circle is being structured. That means it becomes differentiated—a creation procedure is taking place. The circle (female) is fertilized by three lines (male), and something new comes about.

EXERCISE: The Triangle

Now, as the creator of the circle, mark any point on the top of the circle circumference and call it point 9. Then take your compass and, using point 9 as a center point, make a circle with the same radius as your original circle.

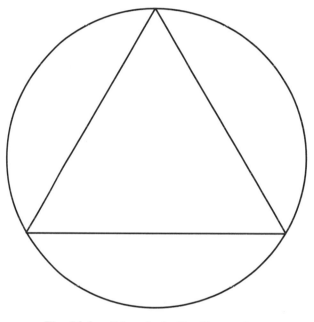

The Divine Triangle in the Enneagram

This new circle intersects the circumference of your original circle at two places, which we'll call A and B. Around A and B, again make a circle with the same radius, and again have two points of intersection with the original circle. Call the point on the right 3 and the point on the left 6. In the last step, connect the points 9, 3, and 6 with each other, and you get an equilateral triangle, which touches your original circle at three points.

With this triangle, you have performed the first act of creation. The three triangle points symbolize:

1. the maintaining and affirming force

2. the destructive and negating force

3. the binding force

That's what Gurdjieff calls the basic forces of our universe, which stand at the beginning of all forms and processes. We might be more familiar with these forces as:

1. thesis

2. antithesis

3. synthesis

Using these three forces, the German philosopher George Wilhelm Friedrich Hegel (1770–1831) described the effect of the world spirit (*Zeitgeist*) in history.

Whether you look at Hegel or Gurdjieff, the Christian trinity or the Hindu, the world is built up through these three forces, which are symbolized through our triangle in the circle. Architect and thinker Buckminster Fuller called the triangle the most important building block of the universe.

The triangle with its point upward, as we have just constructed it, symbolizes the male or generative force. This triangle represents fire, and with it the striving for higher recognition and unity. The scholarly English witch, Lois Bourne, sees in this triangle the symbol of mental concentration.[11]

This triangle draws our attention to the fact that there are three central themes for the human being:

1. the body

2. the feelings

3. the consciousness

The three basic centers of the human being correspond to these three themes:

1. the movement center, out of which the so-called "belly" type lives (mostly)

2. the emotional center, out of which the feeling type lives (mostly)

3. the consciousness center, out of which the mental type lives (mostly).

We can assume that the information-processing part of our brain also follows the law of Three.

THE HEXAGON

Three forces are now at work in the circle and evoke reactions and effects: A strangely entwined hexagon comes about, opening wide downward, as if it wanted to receive the procreative forces of the world. In his unusual language, Gurdjieff calls this figure "the line of the course of the forces—which is interrupted constantly and whose ends combine again." He stresses the fact that this irregular hexagon reflects the inner logic of the forces that go into the making of all events. When the hexagon is in place, it forms a line—1, 4, 2, 8, 5, 7—which is also called the "line of eternal recurrence" or "line of periodicity," since every process and every event follows this course.

If we follow the line drawings of this hexagon, we are looking at the dynamics of a process. You could also say that the line drawing conveys a deeper sense of the process. So, we can characterize the different sections as follows:

Line drawing $8 \rightarrow 5 \rightarrow 7 \; (\rightarrow 1)$

This view is directed backwards, which we call the aspect of involution. Referred to the human body, this line drawing characterizes used blood.

Line drawing $1 \rightarrow 4 \rightarrow 2 \; (\rightarrow 8)$

This view is directed forward, which we call the aspect of evolution. This line of sight shows us the inner functioning of a process. This line of sight corresponds in the human body to arterial blood.

Line drawing $7 \rightarrow 1 \rightarrow 4$

These three points symbolize the stability of a process.

Line drawing 2 → 8 → 5

This line drawing embodies the emergence and dealing with new events in a process.

EXERCISE: Constructing the Enneagram

The figure that you are going to construct now completes the Enneagram. You can no longer construct it with just a compass and ruler. The creation has progressed, and we are now on a differentiated level. This is also expressed by the fact that now we need a protractor.

First, draw a helping line through point 9 and the center of the original circle. Then measure a 40° angle. Where the leg of this angle intersects the right side of the circle, lies point 1. When you project the angle to the left, you get point 8.

From now on you can use just the compass and ruler. In the next step, take your compass, and using point 9 as a centerpoint, and the distance from 1 to 9 and/or from 8 to 9 as a radius, make a circle with the same radius around point 9 in order to get the points 1 on the right and 8 on the left. Then make a circle around point 3 and one around point 6 and get the points 2 and 4 on the right side and the points 5 and 7 on the left, where the circles intersect the circumference of the original circle.

In the last step, connect the numbers as follows:

1 → 4; 4 → 2; 2 → 8; 8 → 5; 5 → 7; 7 → 1

and the Enneagram is completed.

Now you have the completed Enneagram in front of you, ready for you to meditate upon. In that state, observe this cosmic symbol with open eyes and let it affect you.

You may have noticed:

1. All the points of the hexagon were constructed from three triangle points, since these represent the three basic forces that produce every further differentiation.

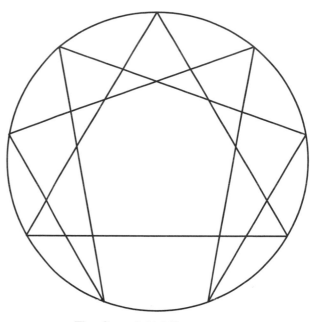

The Completed Enneagram

2. The lines of the triangle and the hexagon are not connected, since they are different levels of forces.

a. The points of the triangle and their connections symbolize the original forces of the creation. Here, forces work from outside into the system of the Enneagram, and therefore these points are called "shock points." At the shock points, the system is open to outside impulses.[12]

According to Bennett's student Anthony Blake, the triangle represents the command-structure or meta-control of a process. Here, commands are given about how the process shall run. At the shock points, sudden and sometimes erratic changes take place, but they are regarded as critical transitions to a new stage of the process.

At the three shock points, the process seems to begin again from the beginning, only starting from a different point. The process continues on a higher level.

Furthermore, these shock points show that the process runs in an orderly way, according to the pattern—showing an "intelligent action."

b. The points of the hexagon symbolize the results of the creation. They are divided by the three shock points into three triads:

Points 1 and 2—aspect of the material creation

Points 4 and 5—aspect of the emotional creation

Points 7 and 8—aspect of the mental/spiritual creation.

The Enneagram points 1, 2, 3, 4, 7, 8, plus the vertex point 9(0,) symbolize the law of the octave, according to which every intelligent process runs. The idea that a process takes place in seven steps is the cornerstone of Gurdjieff's system.

3. The line drawing of the hexagon resembles a labyrinth in which one can always change from the right side to the left, and vice versa in a certain rhythm. But here, in contrast to a labyrinth, you never reach the center point.

In order to better understand the individual points of the Enneagram in the creation model, refer to Chapter 5. There you will find a precise explanation of each point.

You can also imagine the Enneagram as a mandala with three gates. The Enneagram represents a symbol of the form force, which makes the world unfold itself in the way it does. The three shock points of the Enneagram (3, 6, and 9) have to be regarded as the three gates. In front of the first gate at Enneagram Point 3 stands the emotion guard; at the second gate at Enneagram Point 6 stands the mental/spiritual guard; and at the third gate, at Enneagram Point 9 stands the physical guard.

More Exercises with the Enneagram

If you want to continue to play a bit with the form of the Enneagram, try the following exercises, which will show you its geometric structure and help you to understand the Enneagram spiritually.

EXERCISE: The Signs of the Enneagram

Try drawing Enneagrams freehand. You can, if you wish, draw the circle with the compass, but draw the triangle and the hexagon into the circle freehand. Always begin with the triangle as the original force, and then draw the hexagon.

You should be able to draw the hexagon swiftly from each point. Practice that and go through the points one after another—1, 2, 4, 5, 7, 8.

Observe whether you have special difficulties at some points. In order to spiritualize the Enneagram, it helps to draw the lines of the Enneagram speedily without the circle that was drawn in beforehand, and if you want to continue, you can play with this form in several different ways. For example, draw an Enneagram into a square and look at the differences between this figure and a real Enneagram. You can also draw in a spherical Enneagram, one in which the lines of the hexagon and the lines of the triangle are bent. How does this figure affect you?

When you experiment with the Enneagram by drawing, you will certainly notice that you can also see the Enneagram as a combination of three identical equilateral triangles.

You will realize immediately when you combine the Enneagram points a little differently that:

• The first triangle (A) is the one already known to us, formed by shock points 3–6–9.

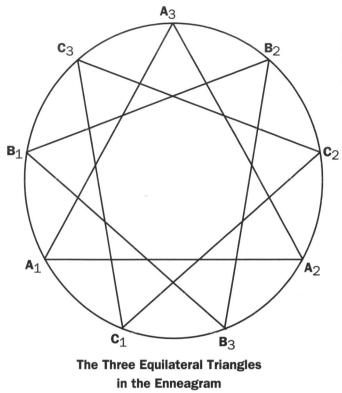

The Three Equilateral Triangles in the Enneagram

Gurdjieff and Bennett describe the Enneagram as a dynamic structure in movement. Imagine it as a slowly turning spiral with point 9 lying all the way at the top and point 1 all the way on the bottom.

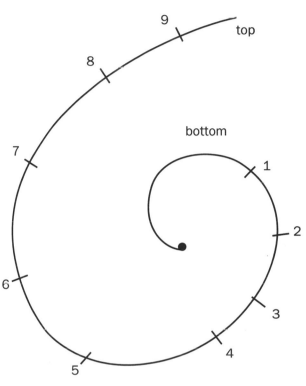

The Enneagram as a Spiral

- The second triangle (B) is formed by the points 1–4–7.

- The third triangle (C) is formed by the points 2–5–8.

You'll see that each third Enneagram point belongs to the same triangle. That illustrates the dynamics of the Enneagram on a symbolic level, because the Three, which is present everywhere in the Enneagram, is considered the symbol of these dynamics.

Now turn the Enneagram very slowly in front of your inner eye. For this imaginative construction you need a lot of patience and quite a bit of practice.

EXERCISE: Visualizing the Enneagram

After you have drawn the Enneagram from different points freehand, you will be so familiar with it that you can visualize it.

To do so, sit or lie down and relax. Close your eyes and imagine the Enneagram as clearly as possible in front of your closed eyes for about one or two minutes.

As you continue to practice, imagine the Enneagram in each case in the three basic colors, red, yellow, and blue.

EXERCISE: Creating the Enneagram in Color

With color crayons, draw, according to your perception, a colorful Enneagram.

You can proceed systematically:

- The color red corresponds to the side of the triangle that goes from point 9 to point 3 (A3–A2), since red symbolizes the material force and the principle of the body.

41

- Points 1 and 2 merge from a pure red into a cold red—which is mixed with some blue.

- At point 3, feeling enters into the system as new energy. Here begins the blue sector, since blue symbolizes the color of feeling.

- The lower side of the triangle—the base—(A1–A2) corresponds to the color blue. You can paint point 4 blue violet and point 5 turquoise.

- At point 6, the second shock point, the spiritual enters the Enneagram as a new quality, symbolized by the color yellow. Therefore, you paint the triangle side 6–9 (A1–A3) yellow.

- Point 7 would become yellow with a fine green tint.

- Point 8 is yellow-orange.

- At point 9, which represents the end and the beginning of the Enneagram, physical energy comes to the Enneagram, which is reflected with a pure red, the color of blood.

Create an Enneagram following these descriptions as aesthetically as possible, and use the image as a pattern for meditation.

EXERCISE: Dream Work and the Enneagram

In conscious dreaming (lucid dreaming),[13] you can move within the image of the Enneagram. First imagine a circle in which you move and which is completely empty. Then, in this circle, the equilateral triangle comes about, and you walk along it consciously and in both directions. Then the hexagon comes about, and you walk along that as well, first in one direction and then in another.

Become conscious of the special quality:

1. of the Enneagram points

2. of the intersections of the Enneagram lines

3. of the two different movement directions in the Enneagram.

Later on, you can visualize a globe coming out of the circle, a tent or a pyramid out of the triangle, and a modern portal out of the hexagon. Experiment with these images and also follow the ideas in your dream consciousness.

The Number Nine as an Essential Structure Characteristic of the Enneagram

"In the ringing of the Angelus, the bell is struck nine times. That happens in order to make conscious the fact that now the eternal energy flows into the field of time."

—*Christian tradition*

"Nine" represents the new. "New" and "Nine" are tightly connected in many languages. In nine steps a process is completed (see page 15), as indicated by the nine steps of Jacob's ladder. The well known magic square (shown here) reveals, in addition, that Nine is the number of the perfect human being, who has developed from body, soul, and spirit, and who is now master of the three worlds.

1	2	3
4	5	6
7	8	9

This magic square, which stems from the Kabbala, can also be seen as the structure model of the Enneagram. The upper row refers to the body, the center row to the feelings, and the lower row to the consciousness or the spirit. So, you can read this magic square in regard to the Enneagram as follows:

- points 1, 2, and 3 belong to the physical level

- Enneagram points 4, 5, and 6 belong to the feeling level

- Enneagram points 7, 8, and 9 belong to the consciousness level.

You may find out for yourself or look it up in my introduction to the Enneagram according to Gurdjieff[14] how the Enneagram in its wings, its right and left side, and its horizontal sections always result in the number Nine.

* * * *

In any case, the Nine is present on each level of the Enneagram. It lends this cosmic diagram not only its name, but also its structure. Special about the Nine is that it symbolizes the indestructible and thus the divine core of the human being. Mathematically, this is expressed in the fact that, no matter what number we use to multiply the nine or raise it to a higher power, it always remains itself (9 x 2 = 18, 1 + 8 = 9, and so forth). Therefore, it is called "the horizon of the numbers" in the *Kabbala* and regarded as the number to which all other numbers lead.

Revealing what the contemporary German Kabbalist Heinrich E. Benedikt writes about the Nine, it seems astonishingly like a description of the ninth Enneagram point:

"The Nine forms the highest force in the human being. To achieve it means to express a divine love. Here the Ego is weeded out, the personal will is fused with the divine. Here the human being has achieved his victory over all his weaknesses and his low impulses. He has brought the harvest home … the Nine is also the fruit of the tree of life, the fruit of the long way through substance, through change, purification, redemption up to the resurrection and to eternal life…. The Nine is the number of love and serving. It owns all experiences, the pleasures and sufferings of the development of the human being as well as the fruits and gifts of the Nine. Thus it shares at the same time understanding and perception with [all creatures], those who suffer and those who are entangled in life, as well as pleasure, wealth, and inspiration with the purest creatures of the higher spheres."[15]

It is astonishing how precisely this quote describes the path through the Enneagram and its goal. That has to do with the fact that the Nine as a structure model represents an archetypal symbol for the force of completion. The Nine symbolizes nine basic consciousness stages or, as consciousness researcher Timothy Leary expressed it, nine switch-circles in our brain, with which we recognize reality.[16] Anyone who reads Gurdjieff's later works attentively will come across references to the Three and the Nine again and again.

For you to recognize the importance of the number Nine for the Enneagram, I would like to guide you in some geometric play.

EXERCISE: Playing with Geometry

When you work with regular geometric figures, and with the nines-division of the circle, a regular nonagon—a star with nine points and nine sides, also called an enneagon—is created in the center of the Enneagram. The number Nine always remains true to itself.

Beginning with the equilateral triangle, which we already know from the so-called shock points of the Enneagram (3, 6, and 9), make a circle with a radius of any size and divide the circumference into nine equal sections. Number the nine points, as you do in the Enneagram, running to the left, from 1 to 0, with 9 forming the highest point. Now draw into the circle a regular nonagon consisting of three equilateral triangles that intersect each other. Beside the triangle 3, 6, 9, a further triangle—1, 4, 7—and a third—2, 5, 8—come about. These three triangles are identical.

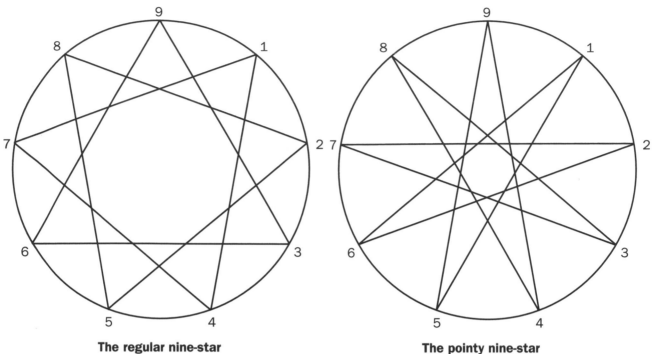

The regular nine-star   **The pointy nine-star**

When you look at the points of intersection inside this nine-star, you find a regular nonagon, in which you can again draw an Enneagram.

You can use this drawing for meditation and think about what the points in each of the three triangles have in common.

When you imagine the Enneagram as a movable figure—as Gurdjieff stresses again and again—the points 1, 4, 7, or the points 2, 5, 8, can also be regarded as shock points, at which a new impulses can enter from the outside into the process.

When you start playing with these thoughts, the dynamic viewpoint of the Enneagram will become more graphic and clear.

Now, turn to a new drawing. Again divide a circle into nine equal sections, and number them according to the Enneagram, running to the left from 1 to 9. This time you connect the 9 with the 4 and then continue to go via 8, 3, 7, 2, 6, 1 to the 5, which you then connect with the 9. Now you have created a pointy nine-star.

Inside the regular nonagon, you will find a smaller nonagon, into which you can again draw the Enneagram.

When you draw this figure, it will strike you that you are always moving alternately in five—and four—steps:

$$(9 \rightarrow 4 \rightarrow 8 \rightarrow 3 \rightarrow 7 \rightarrow 2 \rightarrow 6 \rightarrow 1 \rightarrow 5).$$

How would you characterize this path through the Enneagram points?

The longer you occupy yourself with the Enneagram, the more answers you will find to this question.

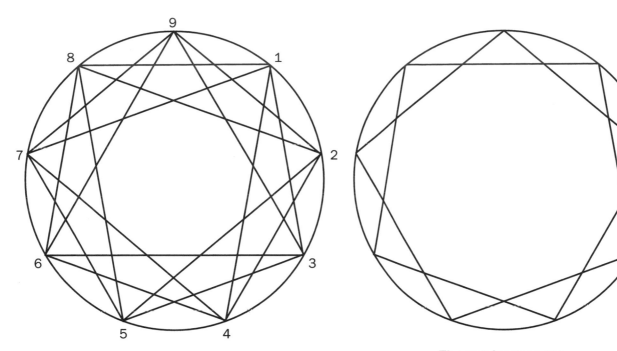

The nine-star, created with 9 trapezoids **The regular nonagon**

Now you come to a more difficult task—creating a nine-star through nine trapezoids of the same size.

Again you draw a circle divided into nine equal sections and numbered according to the Enneagram. Draw into this circle the following nine trapezoids, whose corners form the following Enneagram points:

$$1, 3, 5, 7$$
$$1, 3, 5, 8$$
$$1, 3, 6, 8$$
$$1, 4, 6, 8$$
$$2, 4, 6, 8$$
$$2, 4, 6, 9$$
$$2, 4, 7, 9$$
$$2, 5, 7, 9$$
$$3, 5, 7, 9$$

You cannot draw more trapezoids of the same size into a nine circle. Each Enneagram point now forms a corner of four different trapezoids. The nine-star, with its entwining form, is reminiscent of many patterns from Islamic art.

When you look at the inside of this figure, you will again discover a regular nonagon, into which you can draw an Enneagram, as in the illustration above.

In order to make the form of the regular nonagon even more clear, connect every second point with each other. You will thereby in one line drawing, get to a regular nonagon, which we also know from Islamic art, particularly from architecture.

This figure forms itself in the inside of all the figures that you have drawn up to now. Do you recognize it?

Commentary

All these regular nonagons can be constructed around an Enneagram, their inner intersecting points coinciding with the Enneagram points.

When you regard these different figures as different possibilities, then it will become clearer and clearer what is meant by the dynamic structure of the Enneagram. It is only Oscar Ichazo, with his personality types, who considers the Enneagram to be a rigid figure. In contrast to him, I want to show you the many movement possibilities and the potential paths in the Enneagram.

All the regular nonagons here show an Enneagram (a nonagon) in their center. For me that expresses the idea that all life runs cyclically, as eternal recurrence. What we find in the large nonagon is also formed in a small way in the inner Enneagram. This is a symbol of the mechanical repetition of eternal sameness, which we want to step out of with the application of the Enneagram.

The Enneagram of the Lower and the Enneagram of the Higher Human Being

Until now, we have spoken only about the Enneagram of the higher human being, and we shall continue to do so in the rest of this book. When I speak of the Enneagram in general, I am always referring to the higher human being ("higher" meaning more conscious). But beside that, there is also an Enneagram of the lower human being in the esoteric teachings of the Fourth Way.

But I find the division of human beings into higher and lower very dangerous, because it can only too easily provoke misunderstandings. The French teacher of the Fourth Way, Boris Mouravieff, calls the higher human the "adamic human being," that is, the human being of the eighth (!) day of the creation who, as Friedrich Nietzsche might have said, is stretched between two poles, that of the animal and that of the super-human being. The human being is capable of developing his consciousness systematically. The "pre-adamic human being" is set against this.

This human being is created only from dust and, for him, further consciousness development is not possible, since he did not receive, like Adam, the breath of life from God.

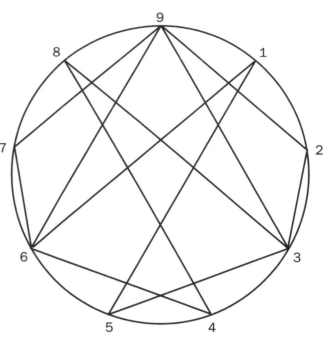

The Enneagram of the "pre-adamic" human being

The pre-adamic human being lived by coincidence, which is easily recognizable in his Enneagram. His Enneagram seems to be undeveloped: It lacks the symmetrical geometry of the Enneagram of the adamic human being. Yet, with the connection of the Enneagram points 9 and 3—and 9 and 6—the divine breath is already indicated, formed by the so-called divine triangle 9 - 3 - 6. This pre-adamic human being is seen as the first step toward today's humanity, a human being who did not show any individuality, which is reflected in the undeveloped form of his Enneagram. He is not yet organized or, in the language of Mouravieff, "fully crystallized," which means that he has not yet developed to his full potential.

I do not want to go into any further details about this distinction between a higher and lower human being, since such esoteric ideas are easily abused (for example, the term Aryan race, as used by Alice A. Bailey, was so misused politically).

5. The Individual Points
of the Enneagram

The statements in this chapter in regard to the individual Enneagram points are clearly divided according to a pattern:

1. The first two pages about the individual Enneagram point present the original Enneagram, as I understand it, as a process-oriented model. There, you will find everything that you want to know about the Enneagram for the comprehension of processes.

2. The next five columns go into detail about the personality types of the Enneagram, which have become so popular in recent years. It is necessary to distinguish Ichazo's personality types from the understanding of the Enneagram according to Gurdjieff.

3. The following six columns examine the Enneagram in relation to other well-known systems that are used to understand the human being and his environment. Here, especially, the color theory of Goethe, East Asian ideas about the energy centers of the human body (chakras), astronomy and astrology, play an important role.

4. In addition to that, you will find a table that summarizes all the important aspects of this Enneagram point once again. Key questions for you to answer form the conclusion. With the help of these questions, you can easily determine how strongly you are inclined toward each Enneagram type.

Even though I am of the opinion that the real strength of the Enneagram lies in its dynamic, process-oriented workings—and not in its relatively rigid personality types—I have nevertheless given a good deal of space in this book to the different types. Since that typology has made this cosmic symbol so popular in the last years, and since it has opened the door to the Enneagram for most readers, I think it is important not only to discuss the types in detail, but also to place them in a dynamic context.

Due to the fact that the teaching of personality types is often flat and undifferentiated, as discussed by Don Richard Riso and particularly also by Richard Rohr and Andreas Ebert—in the last years, first in the U.S. and now in Europe—a general rejection of the Enneagram has come about. It is important to me to show that the Enneagram has a lot more complex aspects than are talked about in most of the books and workshops on this subject. Through this often frighteningly superficial conveyance of the Enneagram, the work with this symbol has become a short-term fad, which does not leave further effects behind. A differentiated and dynamic teaching of types can not only help us to create our lives more effectively and consciously, but it also provides a consistent, practical, and theoretical basis for the understanding of ourselves and of the situations and developments we are experiencing.

About the Personality Types

In the teaching of types in the Enneagram, it is important to understand that there is not only one view of the world. Every type represents a special understanding of it. Certainly

THE INDIVIDUAL POINTS OF THE ENNEAGRAM

you have already witnessed this: You are together with others in a certain situation, for example, and you are stunned that they react so differently than you do. That is due to their different view of the world and to the fact that these others belong to another Enneagram type.

When you study the following tables, it will become clear to you how differently people can see the world and react to it. The more you understand the different types, the more you remove yourself from being a mechanical human being who knows only one way of reaction, which he applies again and again. The purpose of the following tables is to free you from the compulsion of mechanical reacting. Furthermore, the understanding of the different Enneagram types will help you to comprehend social situations faster and to understand the differences among people.

How Can You Make This Teaching of Types Work for You?

You can only begin with the Work at a level of consciousness where you have come to understand your type through self-observation.

Before you are conscious of your mechanical resistance, you will not succeed in opening up to higher consciousness. When you have found your type, it will become clearer to you:

1. what you need to direct your attention to

2. to which fields of actions and feelings you should invest more consciousness energy.

The understanding of your Enneagram type wakes you up from your sleep, and creates a consciousness for your shadow side, and for your wishful thinking. Therefore, many people take issue with the description of the nine defense mechanisms of human beings.

When you read the text about the individual types, let yourself be touched by them. These are not one-sided, intellectual recognitions. The study of these types will make you realize that you are *not* as free as you think. This understanding of your limitation can spur you on to work more consciously and directly toward freedom.

48

ENNEAGRAM POINT 1

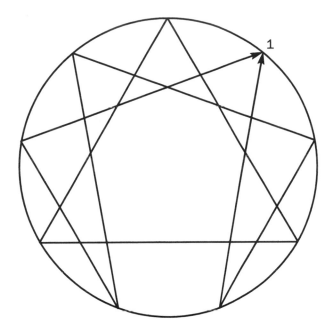

General Characteristics of this Enneagram Point

The first Enneagram point is not only the starting point, but also the place of new beginnings. Here Type 1 is turning to a new challenge, but to get to this level, he first needs to work with his consciousness. At the former level, which got him to where he is now, he has reached the highest degree of consciousness possible (Enneagram Point 9), and now he stands with the first Enneagram point at the beginning of a new level, which again can be run through in nine steps.

In view of this new beginning, he sees at first only surface phenomena and situations, for the most part. Since he has not yet had any experiences at the new level, he is lacking in depth—which after all, is never found at the beginning.

The strength of the first Enneagram point lies in its energy and the drive of the new beginning. These energies of the beginning are absolutely necessary in order to go on and work through the next eight steps of the Enneagram. Here at the first Enneagram point, motivation is built up that helps Type 1 enter into a new process. So it is understandable that this point would correspond to the root chakra, considered in Yoga the place where energy is stored in the human being.

The first Enneagram point represents the child stage of human development. As a child, he is full of energy and fascinated by new things. This often expresses itself through physical activity.

PROCESSES

Processes

Every process begins at this first Enneagram point. Here, the foundations are available for it, and something begins to move or to change. After all, the pre-conditions of this new process were created through an Enneagram that was worked through before.

1. Economic processes

The material foundations for the process are available, or they are now being made available. The economic pre-conditions become clear and you begin to have a hunch about the possibilities they offer.

2. Social processes

Unconsciousness, fantasy, and illusion imprint a situation with which you are very dissatisfied. On the level of the first Enneagram point, you are mostly doing a lot of projecting. You can recognize your own psychological structures only when you are face to face with them. Deep inside, though, you sense the necessity for a change. The time is ripe for new experiences; you feel that strongly.

The first Enneagram point belongs to the level of physical reactions, which—of all reaction possibilities—drains away the fastest. Not rarely, it is illnesses or constant ill health that enable you to begin this process of change. Many of these health-related disturbances may be psychosomatic in origin.

Personal Growth

At this first Enneagram point, the point of the definite beginning, you become conscious of the fact that you are dissatisfied with your immediate situation. It becomes clear to you that you must change something in your life, but you don't really know yet what that could be. Inner tensions and dissatisfaction, though, enable you to take a closer look at your situation and search for the beginnings of a change.

Therefore, you are in a mood in which you are ready to set out on your journey, even though you are only vaguely conscious of where it will take you.

The level of this first Enneagram point is still completely characterized by mechanical (unconscious) actions and reactions.

On this level, you are often occupied for the most part with bringing order into the economics of your life.

EXERCISE: The Beginning

On the level of the first Enneagram point, the following affirmation helps you to experience consciously the state of beginning:

"I take full responsibility for the fact that I am where I am."

Say this affirmation three times a day inwardly, and let it take its effect. You can also use it as a jumping-off place for meditation.

TYPE 1: THE ENTREPRENEUR

Catch Words

Every type has a name that identifies it. Different Enneagram teachers and writers often give them different names. Here are a few of the names for this type, and the writer who coined them.

The ruler (Eli Jaxon-Bear)

The reformer (Richard Riso)

The perfectionist (Helen Palmer, Kathleen V. Hurley, and Theodore E. Dobson)

The entrepreneur (Klausbernd Vollmar)

The beginner

According to Oscar Ichazo, the aggression-impeded idealist and puritan.

Key Words

The point of a new beginning

Primary material

Organizational talent

Addiction to perfection

Fear of poverty

Impatience

Pedantry

Inclination to criticism

Characteristic statement, according to Rohr and Ebert:

"I am right."[17]

General Characterization

Enneagram Type 1 shows a compulsion toward perfection, which can be as intense as an addiction. But he is not only compulsive, but also orderly and overly correct, especially in matters of money. This attitude is characterized by a fear of poverty, which overcomes him quickly. This action-strong Enneagram type, who makes decisions easily, is the most reliable type of the Enneagram. His desire for perfection is expressed to a special degree when it comes to material things. He has fun getting his accounts in order and managing his money in a rather fussy way. At the same time, he has an inclination toward greed.

The Entrepreneur is therefore at the beginning of the Enneagram, because the material things of life play such an important role for him, and because the Enneagram begins with the material segment. He is able to save well, and has a "good feel" for money. The reason for this is that he identifies with his money—which is also his weakness.

The Entrepreneur can decide and act in a flash in an astonishingly confident way. He is impatient and likes to criticize and moralize, especially when it involves business. On the other hand, he is a good businessman, whose strength lies in working independently, and a merry person, as long as he has economic success.

The first Enneagram type lives in the tension of:

1. Striving for security and fear of poverty

   and

2. Suppressed aggression and open fighting.

Strength

This Enneagram type knows about the material needs of the human being, and he searches for inner and outer security. His organizational talent is characterized by the longing to achieve perfection at least in material things. He wants to see situations, human beings, and things in order and well organized. That is the contribution of this Enneagram type on the way to spiritual growth. He meets the demand, which Gurdjieff views as essential for the spiritual development of the human being—for example, to execute each task that he takes upon himself 100 percent. In doing this, he becomes immersed in his task and forgets that his work should be seen only as a game, because otherwise it is too easy to forget himself. That is a hard lesson to learn for the Entrepreneur, who likes to identify with his businesses and his economic success.

In the classical concept of personality types, the Entrepreneur is considered the idealist of the Enneagram. As he once pleased his parents, so he still tries as an adult to be good, successful, and as perfect as possible. If he succeeds in doing this with a serene tranquility, then he is a pleasant person who is well liked by everyone, who goes fairly harmoniously and smartly through life. Yet, this first Enneagram type rather *runs* through life—he doesn't *walk*. Speed is his metier. Through speed, he tries to master the subject. He can act immensely fast and with such confidence because his reality is not clouded by fantasy or illusions.

Some of the most essential strengths of the Entrepreneur are:

1. his knack for business

2. his pronounced organizational talent

3. his striving for perfection

4. his reason and clear view of reality

5. his optimism (in the case of economic success).

Weakness (the Shadow)

Since the first Enneagram type always had to play the good boy or the good girl, a repression of aggressiveness has come about. He doesn't allow himself to express it, since he fears that he would immediately lose his economic success and all recognition and love if he did. Such suppressed aggressiveness explodes in sudden fits of anger and fury that seem entirely out of place in his environment. The Entrepreneur hates himself for these "slips," instead of accepting them and acknowledging them as part of his personality. His shadow is his rage, his repressed fury, which he experiences only in his shadow self.

Rage and fury as an uncontrolled, emotional state make the Entrepreneur blind. He does not see that actions born of rage are not suitable as a means for change.

What can make him unpleasant as a contemporary is his inclination to rigidity and his fears of economic loss, which flare up at the slightest economic failure.

His fear of poverty can make him greedy once in a while, toward himself and others. The unevolved Type 1 is the miser of the Enneagram. He tries, though, to use his organizational talent so that he always has enough money at his disposal. If he doesn't have enough, chaos breaks loose for him. He gets into a foul mood and becomes a grumbling sourpuss. Through this fear of poverty, the first Enneagram type is very dependent on stress. This inclination is enhanced through his readiness to react fast, which is inherent in his nature.

At the first Enneagram point, not only material things are accumulated, but also pleasure and knowledge.

EXERCISE: Consciousness of Rage

Type 1 can profit from the exercise of the positive fighter. In this exercise, which should become a life practice, he makes up his mind every morning to recognize and look at his aggressions precisely, without wanting to change himself. To do so, the Entrepreneur relaxes as deeply as possible in bed in the morning, before getting up, and then tells himself three times quietly:

"I am today completely conscious of my rage."

If he wants, he can in addition make up his mind to stop his work once in the morning, at noon, and in the evening each day, and get to the bottom of how he feels at that moment. If he succeeds in becoming conscious of his rage daily, then he may also make up his mind, with the help of an affirmation, to actually express this rage. It is very important, however, that the Entrepreneur show his partner or friend that the rage is his own, and not project it onto the other person. That means he needs to be completely open with the other person, and reveal how furious he is.

It is vital for him to realize that the other person will not withdraw his affection after that. That is a necessary experience for Type 1. At the same time, he needs to make clear to himself that he will be able to go through life much more securely and pleasantly with this realization.

Since everyone has a part that is Type 1 inside them (which you can see by the repression of aggression in our society), this exercise is useful for many of us—not Enneagram Type 1 alone.

Chakra

Our grounding and our basic life energy stems from our root chakra, which the Hindus call the "Muladhara-Lotos." This chakra gives us the energy to start the day in the morning, and to keep on through the day. On the level of the root chakra, material survival is at stake, as is the material organization of our life. We are, according to Gurdjieff, here in the material part of the Enneagram, where the life basics are created, and upon which everything else is built.

EXERCISE: Grounding

How can you activate the life energies of the first Enneagram point?

Here all grounding exercises present themselves. The simplest one of these is done first thing in the morning after you get up. It begins by placing your feet straight on the floor, close together, and closing your eyes.

At first just feel the floor underneath the soles of your feet. Then imagine that you are getting your breath—when you breathe in—from deep in the earth. Let it flow back deep into the earth when exhaling, taking with it all your tensions, fears, and aggressions. After a while, you will start to stagger. Now imagine that roots are going out from the soles of your feet, roots that reach deep into the earth.

Commentary

Play with this exercise. When you do it daily on a regular basis, three to five minutes a day, it will soon make you feel more grounded in your everyday life.

EXERCISE: Breathing

Furthermore, it helps, at the first Enneagram point, to breathe deeply into the end part of your spine. There, according to Hindu tradition (and also according to the European tradition) life energy rests in the root chakra. Breathe into your coccyx and let it become warm.

Color

The color that is allocated to the first Enneagram point is violet.

Violet corresponds to this first Enneagram point because it represents the color that has stepped out of the invisible—the ultraviolet—into the visible. Violet got its name from the flower, about which there are many songs due to its being the messenger of spring or the "flower of the beginning."

According to a second possible allocation, the color of the first Enneagram point would be red. With red, blood and fire are connected, and both can be seen as energies of the beginning. That is already expressed in the rainbow, which begins with the color red. Like violet, red also stands at the transition to the invisible—namely, to infra-red.

Rohr and Ebert take on the Jesuit color allocation, which, for reasons that are incomprehensible to me, suggests the color silver.

COSMOLOGY

Astronomy

At Enneagram Point 1, stands Mercury, the planet closest to the sun, and the one that moves fastest of all the planets. All teachers of the Fourth Way point out that the beginning of the Enneagram is characterized by the greatest speed. That is because we are in the first section of the Enneagram, in the area of the physical. Our body center reacts fastest to new stimuli.

Astrology

Mercury, god of the merchants, who deals with movable matter, stands at the first Enneagram point. Actually, this force of the beginning, Mercury, is not a god yet, but only the messenger of the gods. But Enneagram Point 1 is so caught up in matter that the divine becomes visible only indirectly. According to mythology, Mercury is able to act, just like the first Enneagram type, astonishingly fast, and can adapt quickly to all the requirements of the environment.

As a sign of the zodiac, we find Taurus here, which symbolizes, as does violet, Springtime. Taurus is an earth sign, with emphasis on the body, marking the material, physical beginning of the Enneagram. This sign has the reputation of being smart in business, which also clearly characterizes the first Enneagram type. For the Taurus as well as for the Entrepreneur, facts count—and nothing else. Taurus also knows the fear of poverty of this Enneagram type only too well.

Animal Symbols

The ant, as an industrious animal and big organizational talent, is allocated to the first Enneagram point, as well as the bee, which is also looked upon as industrious and well organized.

In addition to that, there is the shadow of the first Enneagram point, which is symbolized by the barking and aggressive terrier.

Personalities

Uncle Dagobert, the avaricious and money-grubbing cartoon figure of Walt Disney, personifies this type in its unevolved form. The jovial entrepreneur, as he is often depicted in the cartoon, symbolizes his freed form.

This Enneagram type is ideally personified by the philosopher Aristotle (384–322 B.C.), a pupil of Plato, who, in his intensive and exact nature studies, accumulated a great deal of empirical knowledge that was accepted all the way into the Renaissance. Furthermore, Aristotle, as a typical Entrepreneur, organized scientific terminology and thus created a technical language that is still used today. He was very active, and, during his lifetime, very successful. It is said that he wrote about 170 speeches containing his beliefs, though only 47 of them have been preserved.

Country

The principle of the first Enneagram point corresponds to Switzerland, because it administers money from all over the world, and the principality of Liechtenstein, considered the European tax paradise.

Astrology
Mercury
Taurus

Color
Violet and/or red

Chakra
Muladhara—the root chakra

Kabbala
Chochma or Malkuth
Chochma is the practical wisdom that Enneagram Type 1 is constantly searching for.

Bach blossoms
Vervain[18]
Heather as the blossom of the seventh Enneagram type (the relief point of Type 1)

Body
Digestion

Feeling for Time
The Entrepreneur feels driven by time—even if there is no reason for it. "Time is money"—a Type 1 could have invented this statement. He works constantly against the clock, but is capable of keeping up his concentration for a long period of time. When the Entrepreneur becomes stressed at having to work under time pressure, then a depression-like irritation shows up. He reacts especially aggressively to chatter and unnecessary interruptions. The Entrepreneur wants to make the best out of the present.

Key Questions

(The more questions you answer with yes,
the more pronounced is your resemblance
to Enneagram Type 1.)

1. Do you often fear being impoverished?

2. Are you annoyed with co-workers who do not carry out a task 100 percent?

3. Are you very precise in regard to little details?

4. Are you occupied with your money most of the time?

5. Do you like to work and make decisions independently?

6. Do you think that, without you, everything would be upside down in the household or business you're involved in?

7. Do you know exactly what is right and what is wrong in most situations?

8. Are you a good organizer, who wants to improve everything?

9. Is it clear to you, in most situations, what has to be done?

ENNEAGRAM POINT 2

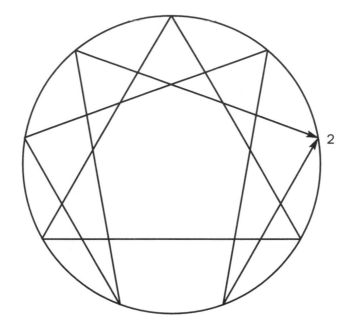

General Characterization of the Second Enneagram Point

The second Enneagram point is the point of the first plan. After the fascination of the new beginning of the first Enneagram point has faded, the energy created—enthusiasm and motivation to change, for example,—must be steered into certain channels in order to work in the desired direction.

At the second Enneagram point, the question arises: What is there to do to use the impetus of the new beginning? How can I employ my energies in order to really create something new?

The second Enneagram point stands in a strange tension between the impetus of the new beginning and the insight that work is necessary in order to use the freed-up energies effectively.

At the second Enneagram point, you begin to have a hunch that an outside impulse (Enneagram Point 3) is necessary in order to make the change, and that you cannot proceed as easily as you thought.

PROCESSES

Processes

The pre-conditions for the process are now being created, so that it can be launched. The work begins, and at least the rough direction is clear. But at the same time it becomes clear that we still must make some changes in the pre-conditions for this process. We realize that we understand much too little about the strived-for process, and we really need further information.

1. Economic processes

Contemplation is needed of the material pre-conditions and how the work force can be organized to best ensure a smooth production process. Production plans are set up.

2. Social processes

You begin to have a hunch that you are projecting all the time and entangled in unconscious, uncontrolled courses of action. You know approximately what you need to change, but you don't know how to remove all the barriers that you have set up to keep yourself where you are. You want to be more conscious, but you don't know how to get there.

Here, as with the first Enneagram point, we are still on the level of the body.

Personal Growth

On this level, the desire for change becomes more intense and clear, and you begin to look for real possibilities of change. You try to analyze your situation, in order to realize where the change will take you. In contrast to the level of the first Enneagram point, you succeed here in developing a perception of your goal.

On this level you are still acting unconsciously for the most part, and are driven primarily by the needs of the body. But soon you realize that you have to get away from this unconscious acting and reacting in order to improve your situation. You don't yet know how it can be done practically. You need more discipline and will power.

EXERCISE: Consciousness of Values

On the level of the second Enneagram point, it is essential that we clarify our conceptions of values, since where you go will depend on them. While you are on this level, place a small card on your desk or in a place where you often sit, with the sentence:

"I will become conscious of my values."

On this level of the Enneagram, it is important to work with devices that assist you in remembering, because it is only too easy to forget our tasks.

TYPE 2: THE PLANNER

Catch Words

The divine mother (Eli Jaxon-Bear)

The helper (Richard Riso, Kathleen V. Hurley and Theodore E. Dobson)

The giver (Helen Palmer)

The planner (Klausbernd Vollmar)

According to Oscar Ichazo: the helpful woman (mother)

Key Words

The point of the first plan

Power of action

Beauty

Manipulation

Female role behavior—dominating through serving

Inferiority feeling

Characteristic statement according to Rohr and Ebert:

"I help."

General Characterization

The Planner, Enneagram Point 2, is the vain connoisseur of the Enneagram. For him, as for Type 4, everything must be beautiful in order for him to feel comfortable, so that he can help and work. He needs as much recognition as possible, in order to satisfy his inferiority complex. If he doesn't get it, he tyrannizes his environment until he does, and he can be really nasty in doing so.

The Planner often reacts like a hysterical person, but he also does lend a hand.

He likes to complain. Here is also a tendency to hypochondria, which becomes particularly intolerable when the Type 2 feels he is not being respected.

He is often attracted by poor and needy people to whom he can convey his vision of a better world. He is very social, for one reason alone—he needs recognition from those around him. Enneagram Type 2, though, avoids any form of neediness himself. He is willing to do others many favors, but he expects gratitude in return; otherwise he reacts crossly. The second Enneagram type seduces or attacks. He very much resembles the principle of Virgo in astrology.

The Planner lives in the tension of:

1. naivete and manipulation

2. recognition and depression

3. aesthetics and suffering.

Strength

Type 2 is mostly charming, lovable, and very active. He can be extremely cordial and arrange everything so that other people and he himself feel very comfortable. He always wants only the best and the most beautiful for himself and for others. He has visions of an ideal world, about which he is enthused and enthuses others; often he can change something. He plans for the future and can also work hard for the realization of his plans. In addition to that, he has an eye for the practical and for things he can make.

The Planner tries to solve problem situations through beauty and elegance.

Weakness (the Shadow)

The unconscious Planner manipulates his environment in the extreme by playing the martyr. Type 2 habitually slips into that role when he is being overlooked and not receiving enough recognition. He wants to make things nice for everybody, and for that he also wants to be rewarded.

This martyr game can be enforced by the fact that Type 2 is occupied constantly with his own, mostly imagined, suffering. When people overlook the Planner, he is absolutely intolerable. More often than not, he reacts hysterically, overexcitedly, and completely inadequately. Even though he is completely realistic most of the time, he must beware of losing his head when in conflicts.

While the second Enneagram type often is very seductive, he is at the same time often very cold in his feelings. Instead of deep feelings, he searches for beauty or dependency in sexuality. He needs very many beautiful partners and has a tendency to exhibitionism. Also in love, the Planner needs constant recognition. At the same time, he tries to form his partner according to his model.

Oscar Ichazo and his successors point out the "helper" syndrome at the second Enneagram point.

EXERCISE: Conflict Situations

It will help Type 2 a lot when he learns to act consciously in conflicts. To do that, he must first become conscious of the situation, because often he does not have any feeling about how to handle conflict situations.

It will help him if every day, in bed in the evening, he would go through the past day and examine where he really reacted inadequately. When these conflict situations become increasingly clear to him, he can try not to act and react that way for the time being, but simply to be conscious of the conflict. That certainly will help to unburden him in the long run.

Chakra

The sacral chakra corresponds to Enneagram point 2. At this chakra, you are dealing with the other one—namely, with the You. This takes place most intensively in sexuality. On a deeper level, with the sacral chakra, we come to the problem of give and take, and into the problem of devotion. These problems represent an essential challenge for the Planner.

EXERCISE: Inhaling and Exhaling

In order to tackle the sacral—or Svadisthana chakra—on the physical level, where we are working, according to Gurdjieff, a breathing exercise is helpful.

Lie down flat on your back and close your eyes in order to be able to listen better inwardly. Breathe calmly and relax. Feel the stream of your breath pass the tip of your nose. When you have found your breathing rhythm, pay attention to whether you put more stress on the inhaling or the exhaling, but don't change your breathing pattern. When we stress the inhaling more, then taking is more strongly pronounced than giving. When we stress the exhaling more, then giving plays a more important role than taking.

If you are a typical Enneagram Type 2, and you notice an over-emphasis on exhaling, it will help to inhale in the next step consciously, and to simply let go during exhaling. Do this exercise for a short time (one to two minutes). When you do it regularly, you can bring your giving and taking into balance.

Color

The color violet is allocated to Enneagram Type 2, as it is to Enneagram Type 1. Violet is a color of darkness—it is the darkest color in the spectrum—and it means that at this stage of the Enneagram, the human being is caught in material matter. Still, a little light of consciousness is present, which will increase with the next Enneagram point.

Rohr and Ebert allocate the color red to the second Enneagram point. As the color of physicality, red corresponds to the first segment of the Enneagram, which is characterized by the laws of matter.

COSMOLOGY

Astronomy

At the first Enneagram point, we find Venus, which is the second planet to orbit the sun. Like Mercury in Enneagram Point 1, Venus shows a periodic change as morning and evening star.

Astrology

Astrologically, the second Enneagram point is allotted to the zodiacal sign of Cancer. Cancer is the motherly principle of the zodiac, corresponding exactly to Type 2, who likes to mother the people in his environment.

The Cancer can plan well with his pronounced imaginative faculties, but he fears nothing so much as rejection. With these two central statements about the sign of Cancer, we have at once characterized the second Enneagram type.

Venus symbolizes the Planner's need for beauty and harmony, as well as his need for love.

Animal Symbols

The cat is allocated to this second Enneagram point, because of the beauty of its movements.

The donkey, as a restless animal, expresses the shadow of this Enneagram point.

The Jesuits also count the helpless puppy as corresponding to Type 2.

Personalities

You can allocate to this second Enneagram type such different personalities as Mother Teresa (Agnes Gonxha Bojaxhin, 1910–1997), who represents a living symbol of free serving and humility, and Michael Jackson, who works with children, even though some of that may be for promotional reasons.

Also, the second Enneagram point has been allocated to famous Hollywood actors and actresses, like Elizabeth Taylor and Barbra Streisand.

Country

The classical country of the second Enneagram point type is Italy. In this country, aesthetics, vanity, and the mother cult combine to form a lively Type 2 culture.

Astrology
Cancer
Venus

Color
Violet

Chakra
Svadisthana (sacral chakra)

Kabbala
Binah or Jessod
Binah is the sensitive understanding for others and the force of knowledge, which is characteristic for the second Enneagram point.

Body
Lungs (breathing)
Bach blossoms
Chicory
Willow (Blossom of Type 4, as the relief type)

Feeling for Time
Time is seen as a chance for communication with other people. For the Type 2, the only time that is considered "good" or properly used, is the time spent with other people. Furthermore, the time factor plays an important role in planning. Planners want to create the present beautifully.

Key Questions

(The more questions you answer with yes,
the more pronounced is your resemblance
to Enneagram Type 2.)

1. Do you like to help others to achieve their goals?

2. Do you need a great deal of recognition?

3. Are the aesthetics of your workplace of special importance to you?

4. Are you considered a friendly and amiable person?

5. Do you find pleasure in alleviating the suffering of other people?

6. Would you do almost anything so that people find you nice and pleasant?

7. Would you call yourself active?

8. Are you diplomatic and capable of adjusting?

9. Can you submit to your partner with lust/pleasure?

ENNEAGRAM POINT 3

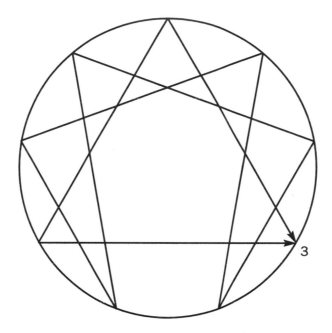

General Characterization of the Third Enneagram Point

The third Enneagram point is characterized by an outside impulse, which directs the impetus of the new beginning towards the desired goal. The new process would run the danger of coming to a halt without this impulse, since you do not really know at the moment how to continue it.

The outside impulse, which takes place at the third Enneagram point, creates new energies in order to be able to proceed toward the goal. Thus, Enneagram Point 3 is a mediator between the beginning of the Enneagram and its middle part. Work on resistance is appointed to the third Enneagram point.

Enneagram Point 3 is called the "mechanical shock point." From Gurdjieff's point of view, this means that the outside impulse that takes place here is still being taken in with relatively little consciousness. It is being processed mechanically, according to routine behavioral patterns.

PROCESSES

Processes

After the pre-conditions have been clarified and the material basics are on hand, it is important to act on them. If we have concluded the preparation phase, we must go a step further so that the process doesn't stop short. We need a new impulse or a new idea about how we can continue to steer toward our goal.

1. Economic processes

In economic processes, this new idea could be a production idea, a new product, or a completely new course in the production of an already existing product. The production idea characterizes the third Enneagram point perfectly, because it must spring from the material experience with existing production operation, as well as from a fantasy. Matter (first Enneagram point) and feeling (second Enneagram point) must come together here productively, in order to fertilize each other.

2. Social processes

In social processes, an idea is also necessary. A relationship or a group comes to a dead end at this spot and dissolves, unless there is an electrifying idea that gets all the members working again toward a common goal. This idea, according to experience, almost always comes through a friend or a critical person from the outside who draws attention to the missing dynamics of the social process. Shortly before this outside impulse takes place, such groups or relationships often seem as if they are dead.

Personal Growth

Finally you have determinedly made up your mind to change. You also realize approximately in what way you want to change, but you do not know how. You recognize your problems, but you have no idea how to go on to reach your goal. Out of this desperation, you turn to the outside world for help. Through this emotional situation, you open yourself up to support from the outside.

It is hard to say what this help will look like. Often it is a book that leads us onto a certain path, or a therapist, but it can also be friends or drastic changes in our life situation that force us on to something new. In any case, on this level you are brought in touch with a healing way in the remotest sense. Here you find your healing device, whether it is a therapy, exercises, or conversations with close friends. These impulses make it clear what you need to undertake now in order to change your situation and get unstuck.

The best way to proceed at this stage is with some kind of consciousness exercise. Often you become familiar with such an exercise through a Yoga or meditation class. In case you do not have a personal teacher, then I recommend that you do the self-remembering exercise in this book (page 24) regularly.

TYPE 3: THE MAGICIAN

Catch Words

The magician (Eli Jaxon-Bear and Klaus-bernd Vollmar)

The status person (Richard Riso)

The performer (Helen Palmer)

The winner (Kathleen V. Hurley and Theodore E. Dobson)

The maker/doer

According to Oscar Ichazo, the radiating status person, who often lies to himself

Key Words

The point of the energetic outside impulse

Master class manipulation of things and situations

Male role behavior. Career stands above everything.

Success orientation

Efficiency

Fantasy, which deceives himself and others with fair words

According to Rohr and Ebert, the favorite sentence of Type 3 is:

"I have success."

General Characterization

The third Enneagram type is narcissistic and image oriented, say the supporters of Ichazo's teaching. That is, without doubt, frequently his effect on the outside world, but in the last analysis, this Enneagram type is in fact a Magician, who is completely involved in the requirements of the outside world.

This type stands at an essential place in the Enneagram, where the material and the emotional segments meet. He has access to both sides, and thus combines the material world, which seeks success, with the world of inner images and fantasies, which often deceives him.

Under any circumstances, the Magician tries to avoid failure and being considered unsuccessful. He could not survive this disgrace. Thus, the third Enneagram type often plays the role of a competent person, representing himself favorably and, most of the time, successfully.

This type looks for success and blossoms in teamwork. Yet, the Magician shows a frightening tendency to be a workaholic. Due to the fact that he has access to the material as well as the fantasy world, his work is distinguished by its dynamics and creativity. Even though he appears as an unapproachable and impersonal doer, he nevertheless has, in contrast to the first two Enneagram types, emotional depth, which he does not necessarily present to the outside world.

He lives in the tension of

1. Performance/achievement and failure anxieties

2. Reality and illusion

Strength

Type 3 searches for perfection, which he experiences in achievement and success. Most of the time, he is successful, since he is not only pragmatic and works a lot, but is also very capable of using his insight into people's nature and his fantasy. The Magician often becomes deeply engrossed in his work, since he feels at home there, where efficiency and hard work are required. He works extremely effectively and has the strength and vision to build up something. It is a strength of Type 3 that he rarely loses his overview, remaining relatively objective in emotionally difficult situations. Since this Enneagram type can enthuse and carry away others, he is often an important member of the work team.

Weakness (the Shadow)

Many of the positive characteristic features of Type 3 are motivated by a fear of failure. The Magician is not a magician anymore if he cannot master things and situations. Then his self-image and strong self-confidence break down. In order to produce the success he craves, he, as a fantasy person, often makes use of deceit in order to achieve the success he strives for. He believes that he will receive love and attention that way, but it often gives others the impression that he is an insensitive career person.

Enneagram Type 3 is fully conscious of his impression on others and often he can hide his real intentions well. His weak point is a lack of distance from himself. The Magician identifies—and over-identifies—with what he does, and how he presents himself to the outside world. That way, it is easy for him to lose himself, and then he is not a magician anymore. In such situations he appears to be enchanted with himself, with an inclination toward narcissism. We can also see this in the seventh Enneagram type, who resembles the Magician in some ways.

It is striking that Type 3 is less interested in sex and relationship than in career. In sexuality, the Magician is like his totem animal, the chameleon. There is almost nothing to which he cannot adapt.

EXERCISE: The Path of Truth

It helps the Enneagram Type 3 person to become conscious of where he lies to himself and to others. Because, just as this Enneagram type fools others, he also easily fools himself. For that reason, it is important for Type 3 to keep a diary regularly. He should note in the diary what he has done and said on the past day and examine it closely for deviations from the path of truth.

First of all, it is important for him to get a consciousness of how he reacts. He should not try to change, because what you fight against you only make stronger by giving it energy. If he develops through the journaling a consciousness of when he fools himself and others, then his behavior will regulate itself in the long run.

Along with the diary work, meditation will help Enneagram Type 3. It will center him and help him to recognize himself—how he behaves.

In addition, Type 3 necessarily needs distance from his striving for success, and meditation can help him to get it.

Chakra

The navel—or Manipura-Chakra—is allocated to Enneagram Point 3, together with Enneagram Point 4. This chakra forms the focal point of the human body. It is the "Hara" of the Japanese, which is so much stressed in their combative sports. Concentration on this chakra brings Enneagram Type 3 to a sense of grounding, and lets him find his center point. That is important for this Enneagram type, since he is easily guided by outside values, such as, for example, success. It is also vital since he tends to lose himself through his striving and his workaholic behavior.

EXERCISE: Honesty

To practice activating this chakra, lie flat on your back on the floor, close your eyes, and breathe deeply and regularly. Place both your hands on your navel and let it become very warm. Now, relax, as deeply as you can and, shifting your consciousness completely to your navel region, say quietly the affirmation:

"I am honest with myself and with others."

Take about five or ten minutes (no more) for this exercise. Then conclude it by stretching, opening your eyes, and letting this exercise resound. Linger a little bit before you turn back to your work.

Color

The color blue is allocated to Enneagram Point 3. Blue is the color that Goethe said represented the darkness, and Enneagram Type 3 must fight this darkness when he wants to struggle through to honesty. At the same time, blue also indicates the direction of this fight. Blue as a symbol color of the soul shows that Enneagram Type 3 must take care of his soul to a special degree, and that he should not sell himself for the sake of success, like Goethe's Faust.

Meditation on the color blue also helps this Enneagram type, since it relaxes deeply and leads the meditator back to himself again.

According to Rohr and Ebert, the color yellow, which symbolizes his expansive character, is allocated to Type 3. The Magician wants to shine like the yellow of the sun.

COSMOLOGY

Astronomy

Enneagram Point 3 represents, according to Gurdjieff, a very special point of the Enneagram—the first shock point. At these shock points, all of which lie on the triangle, a new quality is introduced from the outside. Here, at the first shock point, stands the earth with her satellite, the moon. Earth and moon lie on the third orbit from the sun.

The earth represents the position at which we are incarnated in order to deal with the Work. In the earth life, this is a matter of success and failure, and Type 3 faces up to this task in a completely earthly way, even if he often goes beyond the goal.

Astrology

At the third Enneagram point, we find the fire sign Leo. Leo symbolizes the principle in the zodiac that goes to the outside world and promises success. Leo wants to shine, like Type 3, and gets the ability to do that through his passion.

With Leo, we enter the fifth house of the horoscope: "That is the area of life impetus, will, and creative self-expression"[19], writes the German symbol specialist Johannes Fiebig. And this fifth house corresponds exactly to the quality of the third Enneagram point, at which a new will, a new life impetus is awakened via outside influences. At this Enneagram point it is a typical experience to meet a teacher whom you attract through your inner situation. You receive a huge impetus through this teacher, at first. Yet, the next Enneagram point, that of Virgo, shows the hard work that lies behind the short euphoria of the Leo principle.

Animal Symbols

The chameleon, which emphasizes the adaptability of this Enneagram type, is considered the classic animal of the third Enneagram type. Furthermore, this Enneagram type is symbolized by the peacock, an old alchemist's symbol of change. This is the change that must take place at this first shock point of the Enneagram in order for the process to continue to run towards the desired goal.

The eagle, considered the highest and most evolved form of the third Enneagram point, can rise above everything and thus hold onto an overview.

Personalities

Many people in this third Enneagram point are successful business people and people in the public eye. Everyone who successfully markets his personality has a clear "Magician" part in him. To Enneagram Point 3, especially, belong politicians like Ronald Reagan and John F. Kennedy, and rock stars like the indefatigable, hard-working Mick Jagger.

Country

The typical country of the third Enneagram point is the U.S.A. The country of unlimited possibilities, it is thus magical—just the right country for Type 3.

Astrology Earth Moon
Color Blue
Chakra Manipura (navel chakra) Hara in the Japanese
Kabbala Chessed or Hod (Chod), even though Hod fits the seventh Enneagram type better. Chessed is the love that has been hurt at the third Enneagram point but which spurs him on to be creative and successful.
Body The death of the body (Gurdjieff)
Bach Blossoms Oak Rock water (belongs to Enneagram point 6, but the relief point is here)
Feeling for Time Time is regarded as a possibility for achievement and as a means to reach that goal. Type 3 loves to make quick decisions and seldom postpones anything. Actually, for him, everything should have been done yesterday. The Magician must learn to take some time for himself. A typical Type 3 always works for future goals.

Key Questions

(The more questions you answer with yes,
the more pronounced is your resemblance
to Enneagram Type 3.)

1. Do you love easy-to-take-care-of relationships, which make few demands?

2. Do you have fun playing with things and situations?

3, Do you have a hard time doing nothing?

4. Do other people think you are "lucky"?

5. Can you present yourself well?

6. Do you often experience yourself as a leader or initiator of a group or of a project?

7. Is it important to you to achieve as much success as possible, as quickly as possible?

8. Would you agree with the proverb, "Every relationship is worth a *taler* (a gold coin)"?

9. Do you not always necessarily stick to the truth?

ENNEAGRAM POINT 4

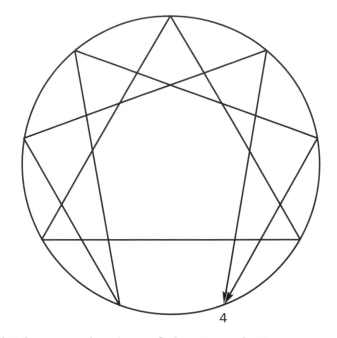

4

General Characterization of the Fourth Enneagram Point

With the fourth Enneagram point we enter the central part of the Enneagram. This center part is marked by the experience of resistance. At the fourth Enneagram point, only difficulties can be seen (at the right side of the Enneagram the perspective goes from point 4 back to the first and second Enneagram points). Through the third Enneagram point, you have become conscious of your situation and now you are being confronted with your own incapacity and lack of discipline.

The transition from the fourth to the fifth Enneagram point is the most difficult one in the entire Enneagram, due to the geometry of the Enneagram. Why—at the fourth Enneagram point—do you tend so easily to fall back to the second and first Enneagram points?

The fourth Enneagram point can be called the crisis point of the Enneagram.

PROCESSES

Processes

Here you know the new way that the process has to be organized so that it will continue in the desired direction. But now unexpected difficulties arise. The process shows resistances and threatens to run in the wrong direction. You need to be extremely watchful here and observe the process constantly; otherwise there is danger that it will run in the wrong direction.

1. Economic processes

In economic processes, at the fourth Enneagram point, frequently a sudden lack of capital occurs. The new work organization was more costly than expected. You need, for example, more personnel or technical devices than planned—or the competition is marketing a similar idea.

If you deal with this situation with consciousness, it can lead to great economic successes. Yet, there is always the risk of interrupting the entire production process and falling back on old, so-called tried-and-true methods. You often do not realize, at this point in time, that in this understandable but dangerous attitude lies the peril of stagnation of the whole enterprise.

2. Social processes

The relationship, the group, or the community are afflicted at this point, often by great inner tension. The people do not get along with each other anymore, and are impatiently waiting for something to change. Nothing changes, but you can win a consciousness about your own laziness and that of the group. This is the point at which many groups and relationships break apart. You have the feeling that you have been striving for a change in vain, and the fact that nothing is happening now shows you that all these endeavors make no sense anymore. You give up.

You would grow and interrupt the repetition of mistakes at this point, especially in relationships, if you would continue—especially here—and tolerate the pressure somewhat longer.

Personal Growth

At the level of the fourth Enneagram point, you are confronted with enormous inner tensions. Enneagram Point 3 offered the key to making the desired change, but at the fourth Enneagram point, you realize how difficult it is to really change yourself. Necessary exercises and regular attention cause a lot more difficulties than you had originally imagined, and you despair at your incapacity to work in a disciplined way towards a change. In addition, you often look back, according to the perspective of the Enneagram, and see that the biggest difficulty of all is to keep yourself from falling back into old ways of behavior.

The situation is very clearly explained by Buddha in the second story of the "Jakata" collection:[20]

A caravan is led by a guide through the desert at night. The guide lies on the first wagon and lets himself be guided by the stars. They make good progress, and before the last night, they drink all their remaining water. That night, the caravan guide falls asleep, and the caravan goes in a circle, through which they all die.

It is through this falling back into sleep that a circular motion comes about, which causes them all to perish. That is exactly the danger at Enneagram Point 4, that you will give up too early and because of that, fail to reach your goal, falling back again into sleep (unconsciousness). This crisis point of the Enneagram is one you simply have to get through, even when everything seems hopeless. Through the enormous emotional tension at this Enneagram point, you can learn everything you need to know to move further on your way and especially to endure tensions, which will be very important for the road before you. Only when you consciously experience these tensions can they be dissolved and changed into something positive—into consciousness, for instance.

EXERCISE: Stability

In order to stabilize yourself at this crisis point, it helps to write down in a meditative, calm state, everything that you want to achieve. Make yourself a detailed list in which you jot down everything you want, without any kind of evaluation. After you have made this list, read it daily. After you read it, imagine for about three minutes that you have already reached all those goals.

TYPE 4: THE AFFLICTED PERSON

Catch Words

The artist (Eli Jaxon-Bear and Richard Riso)

The romantic—formerly the Tragic Romantic (Helen Palmer)

The individualist (Kathleen V. Hurley and Theodore E. Dobson)

The afflicted person (Klausbernd Vollmar)

According to Oscar Ichazo, Type 4 is the complaining, misunderstood artist, who frequently lapses into envy.

Key Words

The crisis point of the Enneagram

Creative loner

Moody, emotionally unstable

Envious

Favorite thought of this type, according to Rohr and Ebert:

"I am special and different."

General Characterization

This type is the most creative and the most genuine lone wolf of all the Enneagram types. The fourth Enneagram type avoids any kind of commonness, whenever possible. He feels he is something special and extraordinary, and he often shows it only too directly to the outside world, even when he thinks he is making it known subtly. But behind this is not the usual search that the Type 4 makes for what is genuine. The Afflicted Person is highly sensitive and knows immediately what is genuine and what is not.

Type 4 is seen by other Enneagram types as being moody and unstable, and they believe that is why they often have difficulties in living and working with him. He is predisposed to be fearful (phobic), timid, and strongly emotional.

"Afflicted people" think of themselves as getting the short end of the stick, and they think that other people (unjustifiably) have more luck than they do. That makes them obsessed with competition, but also unhappily romantic.

The favorite sentence of Type 4 is:

"Nobody understands me."

He lives in the tension of:

1. The extraordinary and sentimental

2. Light (the greatest happiness) and darkness (the most terrible doubts).

Strength

Type 4 brings intuition and sensitivity into the Enneagram. He has a feeling for people and situations, as well as for dealing with the most unusual materials. He usually lives in a very aesthetic environment, which he can, wherever he is, furnish quickly—similarly to Type 2. The Afflicted is usually dressed tastefully, and is a master of symbolic communication. Fours are always extremely emotional types, and can lure the emotionality out of other types with whom they associate.

The Afflicted often inspires other people.

Weakness (the Shadow)

One problem of the fourth Enneagram type is his reserve. He always seem to be harboring a secret. Other Enneagram types have the feeling that they can never understand Type 4 correctly. He is dependent on his feelings to such an extent that he is moody most of the time and emotionally very complicated. He tends to sudden outbursts of rage, spontaneous thoughtlessness, and hard judgments. In addition to that, he is said to be jealous—at least, he thinks that others have it better than he does, and he is misunderstood anyway. But it is probably not the jealousy that bothers him, but a chronic dissatisfaction with what he has. The Afflicted loves the unattainable, which often encourages him to become melancholic. For self-protection, the Enneagram Type 4 often rejects, in a presumptuous and arrogant way—all ordinary things. It is extremely important for him to be special.

Women of this type rather want to be men. Type 4s reveal unusual sexual behavior. As a Type 4, you love the other person with all your heart only when he or she is unattainable. Yet, all Afflicted people, whether men or women, are strongly expressive sexually, and therefore have the effect of being sexually desirable.

EXERCISE: Visualization

The Afflicted, most often, has an easy time with visualization, since he is extremely talented. The following visualization may stabilize Type 4:

Relax as deeply as possible and in this deep relaxation imagine the value of the ordinary and the normal. Have a close look at it. Now let this image dissolve and visualize yourself. Imagine that you are dressed in an entirely ordinary way, that your hair and your appearance are completely normal. Imagine that you are sitting on a bus or in the subway, communicating with entirely normal people. Now dissolve this image and keep reflecting about this whole thing, before returning to your everyday life.

For a change, when you have time and the desire, draw yourself as an ordinary person, and then place this picture where you will see it daily.

In this exercise, it is important that you track down the normal and/or ordinary part in yourself, a part everyone has.

In this visualization, it is important that you not only see the image as clearly as possible, but that you also feel it physically.

Chakra

In addition to Enneagram Point 3, the navel or Manipura chakra is allocated to Enneagram Point 4. The principle of this chakra organizes our dealing with our emotions, and therefore harmonizes our energies. The Manipura chakra can help the Afflicted a lot.

EXERCISE: Breathing Rhythm

In order to work with your navel chakra, lie down flat on your back on the floor and close your eyes. Relax as deeply as possible and listen in to your body. Sense your body very clearly, especially the spots that are in contact with the floor. Now breathe deeply into your navel. That means you pause between inhaling and exhaling or between exhaling and inhaling. When you have breathed like this for about fifteen to twenty breaths, go back to your normal breathing rhythm, relaxing your belly and the area around your navel.

If you do this exercise regularly once a day, you will harmonize and stabilize your emotions, and identify less with them in the long run.

Color

The color green is allocated to the two Enneagram Points 4 and 5. This color is in a special way connected with the emotions. According to Goethe's theories of color, green is the color that represents the light (yellow) mixed with the color that represents the darkness (blue). You can also express this differently: Green connects our shadow with our bright side. A pure green—exactly in the middle between yellow and blue—symbolizes the harmony of our feelings. In green, our light side and our shadow are balanced; we can live both.

Another meaningful allocation possibility connects the color blue with the fourth Enneagram point. Blue, as the symbol color of the soul, which is as deep as the blue ocean and as endless as the blue sky, stands for human feeling. This corresponds exactly with the Enneagram according to Gurdjieff, since, in his opinion, it is with the fourth Enneagram point that we enter the area of the feelings.

The Jesuits allocate to this Enneagram point the color light violet, which is understandable, since violet is frequently regarded as the symbol color of artistic expression and intuition.

EXERCISE: Harmonizing Your Feelings

It helps for the harmonizing of your feelings when you visualize your belly and navel area wrapped in blue and/or green. Imagine that you are breathing in, with each breath, a green or blue colored cloud, which you channel into the area of the navel chakra. Then exhale green or blue out of your navel. With each breath, your navel chakra becomes a deeper and deeper green or blue. Hold this imagined color at your navel chakra for about ten breaths, and then slowly go back to your everyday life.

COSMOLOGY

Astronomy

Mars stands at Enneagram Point 4 with its complex orbit that expresses the complexity of the feelings of this Enneagram type.

Just as the Mars orbit, fourth around the sun, is hard to comprehend, it is also hard to get to the bottom of the emotional movements of Type 4.

Astrology

Astrologically, we find Enneagram Point 4 at the constellation of Virgo. Virgo addresses exactly what is necessary for the fourth Enneagram type—specifically, his grounding.

Furthermore, it helps the Afflicted to take on the analytical attitude of Virgo, because this keeps pulling him back from his unfortunate entanglement in imagination, confronting him again with the hard facts of reality.

Swiss astrologer Huber says that the Virgo type has work problems, which, quite clearly seen from the Enneagram, come about through his over-sensitivity. Like the fourth Enneagram type, the natives of Virgo are usually rejected and judged harshly in most astrological literature.

Animal Symbols

The pigeon dove, as the sensitive soul bird, corresponds to the Afflicted, as does the sensitive and unpredictable Basset hound, a French hunting dog that looks so strange with its short legs. Furthermore, Type 4 is symbolized appropriately by the thoroughbred horse, which can react with much sensitivity and moodiness.

The oyster symbolizes the enchantment of Type 4, and his being a loner.

Personalities

Especially the poets and philosophers of Romanticism, and all melancholic artists, such as Novalis (Friedrich von Hardenberg, 1772–1801), Franz Schubert (1797–1828), and Richard Wagner (1813–1883) clearly show Type 4 parts. The leading romantic philosophers, such as Friedrich Wilhelm Schelling (1775–1854) and Johann Gottfried Herder (1744–1803) tried in their Type 4 way to comprehend the world from the point of view of their own feelings. Furthermore, the Danish philosopher Søren Kierkegaard (1813–1855) can be called a Type 4. Kierkegaard did not only suffer from melancholy, but he also felt himself deeply misunderstood. He searched in his philosophy for what was really important for his life, and he turned, like Gurdjieff, against gossipers and talkative people. In addition, the big Hollywood stars Charlie Chaplin, James Dean, Marilyn Monroe, Marlon Brando, and artist Andy Warhol, belong to the Afflicted.

Country

France, as the classic country of the Bohemians, is said to be the typical country for the fourth Enneagram type.

Astrology
Mars
Virgo

Color
Green and/or blue

Chakra
Manipura (navel chakra)

Kabbala
Gebura or partially also Tipheret (the ideal allocation to the fifth Enneagram type).
Gebura is the passionate force that characterizes the fourth Enneagram type. It needs to be utilized in such a way that it becomes the force of clear thought.

Body
Blood circulation

Bach blossoms
Willow
Vervain (blossom of the first Enneagram type, which is the relief type of the Afflicted).

Feeling for Time
Time is understood very subjectively and is seen from the point of view of intensity of feelings. The time spent with lovers and friends is time spent meaningfully. It is always given priority in comparison to other obligations.
Type 4 often lives out the past.

Key Questions

(The more questions you answer with yes,
the more pronounced is your resemblance
to Enneagram Type 4.)

1. Do people disappoint you constantly, and do you think that life is basically too hard for you?

2. Are you often misunderstood?

3. Does your partner describe you as moody?

4. Do you love your feelings—and do you feel nevertheless that you are being tossed back and forth by them?

5. Do you often long for your own past?

6. Do you long for what is difficult to reach?

7. Most of the time, do you feel distanced from others?

8. Do people often reproach you with reacting too dramatically?

9. Do you think it is necessary for you to be so preoccupied with yourself?

ENNEAGRAM POINT 5

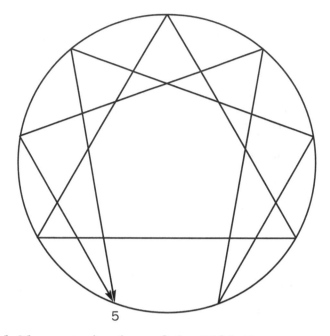

5

General Characterization of the Fifth Enneagram Point

The fifth Enneagram Point has a clear orientation toward a goal. With it, the left side of the Enneagram is reached, which is characterized by the desired goal. The transition from the fourth to the fifth Enneagram Point is the most difficult, as well as the most important one, in the Enneagram, since it takes place from the right to the left side of the Enneagram. The right side of the Enneagram is marked by mechanical and rather unconscious behavior, while the left side of the Enneagram is characterized by developed consciousness and by willpower.

Even though you may still feel far from your goal, you have nevertheless taken the largest and most difficult step in the Enneagram. Yet, the frustration of the fourth Enneagram point still resonates here, expressed by the fact that you feel very far away from achieving your goal, even though it is reachably close before your eyes.

PROCESSES

Processes

Through the experience of stagnation at Enneagram Point 4, we are stimulated to use all our efforts and all our organizational talent so that the process is consistently organized towards its goal. The goal is again completely clear and plainly defined, and the necessary consequences are drawn from that.

You are impatient and annoyed that the process does not run any faster, but that gives you the chance to realize again very clearly where you want to go and what accomplishments and/or sacrifices you will have to make to get there.

1. Economic processes

Changes are probably needed in the means of production or in the production organization. At least, it is necessary to give more thought to the entire course of production in regard to the goal (the ideal product), and bring its individual elements more finely in line with each other.

2. Social processes

In a group, family, or a relationship, you realize where you want to get to, and what you need to do to get there, but what's missing is the elan—the spirit—to do what is really necessary. For that, most of the time, a reorganization of the teamwork or the community life of the group is necessary at the fifth Enneagram point in order to be able to make the required changes more easily. It is important at this stage to realize that even when the social process seems to be stagnating, you nevertheless need to proceed to your goal. You now have gone so far together that you may go the last steps toward the goal together. After having overcome the difficulties of the fourth Enneagram point, you do not need to fear anything anymore.

Personal Growth

At point 5, the worst is overcome. Even though there may not be external progress, the goal is clear before your eyes, due to holding your ground at the previous Enneagram point. Type 5 looks toward point 7 and 8—not back to previous stages. On the level of the fifth point, you suffer from the fact that you cannot proceed faster, but you realize that advances are made only through conscious suffering.

As an emotional person, Type 5 must deal—like Type 4—with his suffering, since otherwise he cannot proceed. For both, the learning exercise consists in not identifying with their suffering.

EXERCISE: Negative Thinking

At point 4 and 5, Type 5 suffers from the fact that he strays back to the past in his thoughts, and that he is preoccupied inwardly in previous crisis situations that had negative events and failures. Through this, he may easily fall into negative thinking, which has to be avoided at this emotionally difficult stage. In order to get around the hindrances that come about through this thinking, you can use some techniques from NLP (neurolinguistic programming) and purify your memories from everything that does not agree with what you want. One way to do that is to make a list, in which you enter all your negative thoughts in regard to success, relationship, money, and everything else that is important for yourself. At each problem, ask yourself, what is the cause of this problem; then dissolve these problems in your imagination. This way, you can in fact free yourself from negative programming, which is one of the most important tasks at Enneagram Point 5. Why not try it?

87

TYPE 5: THE OBSERVER

Catch Words

The mystic philosopher (Eli Jaxon-Bear)

The thinker (Richard Riso)

The observer (Helen Palmer, Kathleen V. Hurley, Theodore E. Dobson, Klausbernd Vollmar)

According to Oscar Ichazo, the retreated thinker who suffers from the meaninglessness of the world.

Key Words

The point of the most important and at the same time most difficult process in the Enneagram.

Reserved to retreated

Objective observer

A lot of knowledge

Action impeded

We could ascribe a popular sentence to this fifth Enneagram type:

"My home is my castle."

Rohr and Ebert suggest this sentence:

"I look through (understand)."

General Characterization

Type 5 represents, along with Type 4, the emotional pole of the Enneagram, even when the Observer hides his feelings behind his intellect, as he often does, because he fears them.

Typical for Type 5 is his paranoid schizoid way of reacting.

He lives in fear of becoming involved in his feelings. Therefore, he flees into analytical thinking and loves systems (many people of this type occupy themselves extensively with the Enneagram, which gives them security).[21] We can also characterize the fifth Enneagram type as one who knows much and acts little. Acting is too dangerous for him, since, through it, he could entangle himself emotionally.

The Observer is confident, with an inclination to British humor, which is often overlooked. He gives the appearance of thinking he is better than everyone else, in order to keep the environment at a distance.

He searches for knowledge; in fact, he is the classic knowledge-thirsty person, and he is always a good teacher. Astonishingly, the observer digests all this knowledge inwardly.

The fifth Enneagram type lives in the tension of

1. Knowledge and action incapability

2. Smartness and shy retreat

Strength

All the other Enneagram types think that Type 5 is shy and retreats into himself—at first. Type 5 often cultivates this attitude even more through his inclination to oddball eccentricity. Also, through his remote manner, the Observer often seems to be British. His reserve and sober distance make it seem that he is a resting place in a world that is hysterically loaded. His manner has something fine about it, characterized by an inclination to subtle humor and analytical sharpness. In addition, Type 5 usually has an intellectual view of the world, which makes it often very informative and pleasant to talk with him. You immediately have the feeling that he has perspective, and that is mostly, in fact, the case. But Type 5 is by no means only an intellectual; he is above all a person of feelings.

Furthermore, he is a master of objective self-observation. His knowledge is therefore not isolated. While he may have acquired it only by reading, he has digested and spiritualized it himself.

You could say about Observers that they are patient in their relationships and loyal. Though they may not always be exciting sexual partners, they are pleasant ones.

Weakness (the Shadow)

The Observer is afraid of getting emotionally involved. Therefore he looks one-sidedly for knowledge and isolates himself from others when he feels threatened. His fairly extreme orientation toward learning does not let his emotions shine through. Unfortunately, though, the knowledge he acquires is not conveyed freely, but is held back, since he needs it for himself. This knowledge is intended to fill an otherwise unbearable emptiness, of which he is very much afraid. This emptiness has sprung from his fear of emotional involvement, which makes him appear emotionally aloof. Yet, he seems to be very emotional, and often somewhat helpless, even where he has confidence.

The Observer does not understand that knowledge wants to be conveyed and expressed—yes, that the universe downright demands that knowledge be passed on and applied!

It is best to elicit knowledge from Type 5 at first in a confidential conversation.

EXERCISE: Expressing Feelings

Calling to mind his feelings helps the Observer like no other Enneagram type. One of the most useful partner exercises for him consists in sitting opposite a partner, looking into his or her eyes, and saying over and over, "I love you," while watching the person opposite him.

This exercise forces even Type 5 to express his feelings, if he only does it long enough (at least five, and at the most ten minutes).

By regularly writing in a diary, Type 5 is forced somewhat more gently to express his feelings. The task is amazingly easy. He needs to write every evening in his diary what he emotionally experienced during the day. He can apply the precise analytical observation —at which he is so skillful in other matters— just as well to himself. That will help him to express the result of his self-observation in writing in his diary. It is helpful for some Observers to begin every entry into the diary with the words, "I feel..."

Chakra

The Anahata, or heart chakra, is allocated to the fifth Enneagram type. According to Sufi teachings, wisdom lives in the heart of the people. This is where Enneagram Type 5 should look—into his heart. He will then realize that he does not need to be afraid of his feelings any longer, and that a wisdom is living in his heart that is far superior to that of his head.

EXERCISE: Heart Meditation

As an Observer, you need to meditate on your heart by perceiving and imagining it as precisely as possible. You will notice that, through the strength of the heart, you finally come to the true wisdom that you strive for.

Start the exercise in deep relaxation, lying on your back. First you will notice how it beats. Then visualize your heart very clearly and accurately, producing a precise image in front of your closed eyes. If you have trouble with this, you can consult an anatomy book and find out exactly what the heart looks like. After that, you will be able to feel it more easily. Next, you need to "feel into" your heart, and let all the feelings and images rise that want to rise. Have a look at them—without trying to change them.

Color

Green is allocated to the fifth Enneagram type. Green is the color of the heart, which forms the emotional focal point of the body. The heart chakra is the center chakra, and therefore also the center of the color circle, so pure green is allocated to it.

The Jesuits, as well as Ebert and Rohr, allocate the color blue to the fifth Enneagram point. Blue, as a classic symbol of the color of the soul, characterizes the center Enneagram section, where it is connected with the force of feeling.

EXERCISE: Heart of the Buddha

Since the heart chakra, like the previous one, lies in the emotional segment of the Enneagram, meditation on the color green helps it. Sit down and keep your spine as straight as possible. Close your eyes and imagine the figure of a Buddha. Once you have a clear image of this figure, visualize with each breath a green light going out from your heart and touching the heart of the Buddha, and then, from the heart of the Buddha, a green light coming out and touching your heart. Hold this image for about five breaths before you go back to your everyday life.

Do not think about this exercise—just do it. The exercise will strengthen the force of your heart in the long run, without you having to do anything.

COSMOLOGY

Astronomy

Jupiter is allocated to the fifth Enneagram point, since it describes the fifth planet in orbit around the sun. Just as the heart chakra forms the centerpoint of all chakras of the human being, so the orbit of Jupiter forms the center orbit of all the planets. At the same time, the periods of its visibility connect Jupiter with Mars (on Enneagram Point 4), and Saturn (on Enneagram Point 6).

Astrology

The constellation Scorpio lies on Enneagram Point 5. This principle of the zodiac reaches down into the depths, and it is exactly that which characterizes Type 5. Both Scorpio and the Observer represent shy, retreated people who are introverted, according to Carl Gustav Jung. The principle of Scorpio has to do with the mystery of death and birth. That characterizes the situation at the fifth Enneagram point very well. The emotional, mechanically reacting human being must die before the conscious human being can be born at Enneagram Point 6. This is the second birth, which is seen in esoteric writings as a necessity on the last stage of the spiritual way. The old, unconscious, and mechanical human being must perish in order to make room for the new conscious being, which marks Enneagram points 6, 7, and 8 as a spiritual segment.

Also Jupiter, who is allocated to the fifth Enneagram point, is seen by the Italian astrologer Roberto Sicuteri[22] as a principle that opens the doors to individuation and higher consciousness.

Animal Symbols

The animal of the fifth Enneagram point is the owl. It is regarded as the symbol animal of intellect, and at the same time as a shy, nocturnal bird. The same holds true for the fox, who is also a smart but shy animal that digs himself into the earth.

The Jesuits also allocate the hamster to this Enneagram point, because it gathers food, just as the Observer gathers knowledge and information.

Personalities

I count all well-informed loners as the Observer type, and all lone specialists in their field, or philosophers: for example, Thomas Aquinas (1225–1274), who observed the paths of belief and reason; René Descartes (1596–1650), who systematized modern philosophy; and the introverted philosopher of man's existence, Martin Heidegger (1889–1976). As a scientist, we find here Charles Darwin (1809–1882), who traveled on the ship *HMS Beagle* from 1831 to 1836—to the coasts and over the oceans, who observed everything precisely and did not publish his ideas until twenty years later.

An anecdote is told about Immanuel Kant (1724–1804), who observed the world from Königsberg, Germany. One day he wrote on the door of his lecture room: "Cannot come today, have not finished thinking yet."

Country

The typical country of Type 5 is Great Britain, the country of "splendid isolation" (perfect isolation "shielded from the outside world") and of eccentrics, among whom you can find many Observers.

Astrology Jupiter Scorpio
Color Green
Chakra Anahata (heart chakra)
Kabbala Tipheret or Chessed Tipheret represents beauty, which is seen in the Kabbala as being speculative and honest. The fifth Enneagram type, who is characterized by this beauty, must learn that Tipheret also has an active side.
Body No allocation
Bach blossoms Water Violet Vine (blossoms of the eighth Enneagram type, the relief type)
Feeling of Time Time is seen as an opportunity for observation and for gathering of information. Since Observers like to think, they are often seen by others as being slow. They are always interested in the past.

Key Questions

(The more questions you answer with yes,
the more pronounced is your resemblance
to Enneagram Point 5)

1. Is it important to you to know and to catch everything?

2. Do you feel inhibited when around other people?

3. Do you know a lot, without having any idea of what you can do with it?

4. Do you often say the sentence,"If only I had stayed home…"

5. Do you like to observe other people?

6. Do you think of yourself as being a profound thinker?

7. Do you frequently hide from others?

8. Can you make decisions best on your own, without getting the advice of others?

9. Do you need a lot of time for yourself alone?

ENNEAGRAM POINT 6

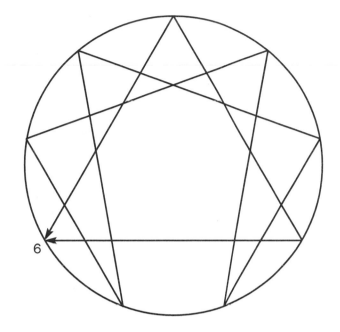

General Characterization of the Sixth Enneagram Point

The sixth Enneagram point is, like the third, a shock point, since an outside impulse now gives the impetus to reach the desired goal. Without this "kick," the process could not be completed.

Most of the time, the sixth Enneagram point brings deep insights or unexpected solutions. This Enneagram point connects the center part of the Enneagram with its last part, and thus creates the transition from a critical area to the goal of the Enneagram.

In contrast to the first shock point at Enneagram Point 3, we search and absorb the outside impulse at this second shock point with a high consciousness. This consciousness is necessary in order to bring the process close to its goal.

95

PROCESSES

Processes

With the sixth Enneagram point, we are at the second shock point of the Enneagram. Only through an impulse from outside do we proceed. At Enneagram Points 4 and 5, we had the feeling that it would not go through at all. This provoking problem in dealing with our goal made us, in the last analysis, look outside once again for help. As before, it is a teacher, a lover or a friend, a book or a therapist, who helps us to go on at this stage. Basically, we only need a little push in order to get to our goal, and this push is given from the outside. If this push does not happen, then the process runs down, and cannot be completed successfully.

1. Economic processes

On the level of the economic process, we have come to the stage where we need to create a harmonious image for our product. The product to be produced—or the offered service—must be regarded in connection with all of society, because at Enneagram Point 6, social presentation is important.

The process, which stagnated at Enneagram Points 4 and 5, is starting to move again, and runs as planned toward its goal.

2. Social processes

In groups of all kinds, we learn at Enneagram Point 6 to recognize our projections as such (most of the time through therapeutic insight). As a result, it is possible to pull back these projections, which has a positive effect on the group situation. Only now can you look at the group and at your own situation in the group realistically. That forms the basis for quickly proceeding toward the desired goal.

Personal Growth

Enneagram Point 6 represents the second—the conscious—shock point of the Enneagram. Here, dependence on the emotions has been overcome, but this doesn't mean that you have become emotionless. At this sixth Enneagram point, you can steer and experience your emotions consciously; that means you can perceive your emotions, but not identify with them anymore. Through this, you can freely decide whether you want to express your emotions or not.

With the sixth Enneagram type, freedom of will comes into play. Until this point, no will prevailed, since you were way too dependent on your own body and feelings. From here on, you are responsible for your actions, because you can decide consciously what you will do.

The psychology and philosophy of positivism rejects the idea of free will. That is understandable, because, from Gurdjieff's point of view, hardly anyone gets up to the sixth Enneagram point anyway.

But, in the tradition of the Fourth Way, it is assumed that the student can reach the second shock point only with a teacher or with a study group.

TYPE 6: THE HERO

Catch Words

The hero (Eli Jaxon-Bear and Klausbernd Vollmar)

The loyal one (Richard Riso)

The trooper—formerly the devil's advocate (Helen Palmer)

The co-fighter (Kathleen V. Hurley and Theodore E. Dobson)

According to Oscar Ichazo: the frightened and doubting human being.

Key Words

The point of the last conscious impetus

Loyalty/faithfulness

Security

Rohr and Ebert have this type saying the sentence:

"I am doing my duty."

General Characterization

This type, according to Ichazo and his successors

The sixth Enneagram type is the most loyal of the Enneagram. It corresponds to the ideal of the loyal servant or the loyal official. "Sense of duty over everything" is his motto. Type 6s need and seek security, which they hope to get through their loyal performance of duty. Enneagram Type 6 therefore avoids misbehavior and can be seen as the most adapted Enneagram type.

But he is also a suspicious doubter, who has big problems with his own decisions—that's why he is often found in large organizations or bureaucracies where he feels comfortable and secure and certainly does not have to make any decisions by himself.

He lives in the tension of

1. Security and anxious doubt

2. Holding his ground and flight

This type, according to Gurdjieff and his successors

The sixth Enneagram type stands at the borderline between the areas of the emotions and the area of the consciousness. He takes part in the suffering of the Enneagram Types 4 and 5, and also in the consciousness clarity that the Enneagram Types 7 and 8 can reach. From this position, Type 6 succeeds in going on his way effectively, with self-determination, and in a serving manner. He is thus also the loyal servant of a special task, which he prescribes for himself. This task was not brought to the Hero from the outside, but he feels connected to it from inside.

Strength

Type 6 is one who creates his own space. The cube has six corners and symbolizes the space at which you collect yourself and come to a rest. The Hero creates exactly this space of security. In a family, an institution, a company, or also a certain task, he is a lovable person who is completely cooperative. Extremely loyal and dedicated to his task, the Hero tries to accomplish it even when faced with the greatest difficulties.

He is always conscious of his duty, and he goes stubbornly, patiently, and resolutely on his own way. He can tolerate conflicts without getting beside himself. He is a person you can trust and you certainly never will be disappointed.

Most of the time, Type 6 succeeds in estimating his situation fairly objectively and acts out of this estimation decisively.

Weaknesses (the Shadow)

According to Ichazo and his successors

Most of the time Enneagram Type 6 is afraid to move into an open position. Highly suspicious, he hides his real opinions and presents only the prevailing thought to the outer world. If the Hero for once has to decide something on his own, which is a horror to him, then his speech is characterized by the conditional ("if that were to happen," etc.). Other phrases common to him are: "it depends...," "Maybe, if it turns out..." "We'll see," and other similar vague expressions. Therefore, it is hard to do business with a Type 6. He often prefers to bustle around in administrative or bookkeeping positions, since he fears decisions above everything. He seeks authority above him, and often lives in bondage to it.

Heroes cannot deal well with originality and often represent a boring average, without self-confidence.

According to Gurdjieff and his successors

The ability of Type 6 to be objective is also his biggest weakness, because he sees himself and others only from a distance. He is, in addition, inclined to look down on his fellow beings with a certain haughtiness. The Hero must be careful not to use his abilities unscrupulously for his own advantage and not to succumb to his own fantasies of power.

EXERCISE: Overcoming Distrust

Type 6 is characterized by the fear of loss of security. He needs to learn that he can give himself the security that he needs for his well-being. An important step in getting to this security consists in overcoming his distrust of other people. To do that, the following partner exercise is very appropriate.

The Hero chooses a partner with whom he can perform this exercise. The partner blindfolds him and then stands behind him. Now, Type 6, after some swaying, lets himself fall backward, whereby his partner catches him as close to the floor as possible. Type 6 should perform this exercise regularly, since it reminds him of the fact that he can trust others, and that he can be secure enough to hand himself over to others.

Chakra

The sixth Enneagram point corresponds, as does Enneagram Point 5, to the heart chakra, which lies opposite these two points in the inner heptagon of the Enneagram.

According to Gurdjieff's teachings, at this second shock point of the Enneagram, the feeling force is converted into a conscious force, and the spiritual force comes into the system, as a new quality. Spiritual force can perhaps be better understood as consciousness force, because at this Enneagram point, the individual is conscious of what he feels and how he acts. That is the wisdom of the heart, described by the Sufis, who see the heart as the recognition organ in which a high consciousness is created. In order to stimulate the heart chakra, and thus to create the transition to higher consciousness, any kind of consciousness exercise will help.

EXERCISE: Negative Feelings

I would suggest, at this Enneagram point, that for one week you do not express your negative feelings, but at the same time be conscious of them. Make up your mind in deep relaxation in the morning in bed, after you wake up, to be conscious exactly of the point at which your feelings change from positive to negative. When, in your everyday life, negative feelings are provoked, do not express them, but instead call *yourself* to your mind. To do that, stop your daily activities and become conscious of your body. If you succeed in doing that, you will realize that your feelings split. There is a part of you that is calm and composed, as it looks at the situation, and another part that is obsessed with negativity. Place yourself consciously on the side of the composed part—that way you can deal far better with difficult situations.

But if you are already sucked into the negative part of yourself, reacting furiously and harboring fantasies of all kinds of revenge, then also stop—as soon as you become aware of the situation—and become aware of the point at which the negativity began. Make yourself aware:

1. at which points you tend to react in a negative way

2. how much energy this negativity takes away from you.

Have a very close look at this, and make up your mind to interfere earlier next time.

Negativity that is consciously unexpressed, lets something new come about inside you, which conveys an inner security and strength. This attitude is not to be confused with the repression of negativity, which happens unconsciously.

Color

The color yellow is allocated to this Enneagram point. Yellow as the symbol color of the spirit, which shines beyond its limits—like Type 6—points to a new quality that comes about at the sixth Enneagram point: the spiritual.

Rohr and Ebert allocated to the sixth Enneagram point the color beige-brown. I can explain the allocation of this color only by the fact that beige-brown is a differentiated mixed color, which emphasizes the complexity of the sixth Enneagram type.

EXERCISE: Purifying the Spirit

It helps at this stage to "breathe yellow color." Imagine, that with every breath, you breathe in a yellow color, which covers your entire body with a yellow translucent light. Hold this image of the yellow body for about ten breaths, and then return to your everyday life. A pure yellow purifies the spirit of all poisons, which make themselves felt as negativity.

COSMOLOGY

Astronomy

At this second shock point of the Enneagram, which represents the threshold to a new consciousness, Saturn stands. It is the guard of the threshold, the last planet that is visible with the naked eye. It rotates around the sun on the sixth orbit.

Astrology

Astrologically, the quality of Enneagram Point 6 corresponds to the sign of Sagittarius. Sagittarius knows how to reach his goal, since he has an overview. He does not let himself be distracted by details; he sees the whole and what is important—an ability that is reached at the sixth Enneagram point.

Sagittarius goes on his way like the Hero, who is characterized in the Enneagram by the fact that he is able to observe his environment fairly objectively.

Animal Symbols

According to the Jesuits, who follow Ichazo, shy animals like the hare, doe, and mouse are allocated to the sixth Enneagram point.

According to Gurdjieff and his successors, though, a more likely animal would be the wolf, who is seen as a smart loner (lone wolf), and who often, in fairy tales and fables, tries to use his power. Also, the rat could be allocated to this Enneagram point, because it is said to be clever.

Personalities

Following the teachings of Ichazo, you can allocate the type personified by Woody Allen in his films to this sixth Enneagram point. Another side of this type is astonishingly well described in Søren Kierkegaard's philosophy under the aspect of the duty-bound person ("the human being at the ethical stage"). This person measures all his actions via higher (authoritative) measurements.

According to Gurdjieff's view, though, I would rather think of personalities like Adolf Hitler (1889–1945) and Vladimir Iljitsch (actually Uljanov) Lenin (1870–1924).

Country

Germany is seen as the typical country of the sixth Enneagram point. One aspect of the image of the German is that he considers himself particularly eager for big ideas.

Astrology Saturn Sagittarius
Color green
Chakra Anahata (heart chakra)
Kabbala Nezach or partially also Geburah Nezach represents perseverance and loyalty, which, after all, the sixth Enneagram type has plenty of. This Enneagram type can learn from Nezach the lively and open side.
Body the end of the dependency on feeling (Gurdjieff)
Bach blossoms Rock Water Wild Rose (blossom of the relief type of Enneagram type 9)
Feeling for Time Time is an authority to which you must necessarily bend and submit. Furthermore, for Type 6, time is only used meaningfully when he is doing something for an authority—that means, when he has executed instructions and commands. The Hero always tries to make the best of the present.

Key Questions

(The more questions you answer with yes,
the more pronounced is your resemblance
to Enneagram Type 6.)

Questions that refer to this type according to Ichazo

1. Have you ever in your life devoted yourself completely to a task or to an idea?

2. Do you think that we can learn something from "the good old days," when authorities were still valid?

3. Is it difficult for you to open up to innovations?

4. Can you not tolerate rejection or criticism?

5. Do you fear excesses?

6. Do you tend to react fearfully and cautiously?

7. Do you prefer to get advice from friends or co-workers before making decisions?

8. Do you think of yourself as being correct?

9. Can you fit well into groups?

Questions that refer to this type, according to the schools of the Fourth Way

1. Do you react in conflict situations with flight forward?

2. Do you have the feeling that you know yourself?

3. Do you frequently have fantasies of power?

ENNEAGRAM POINT 7

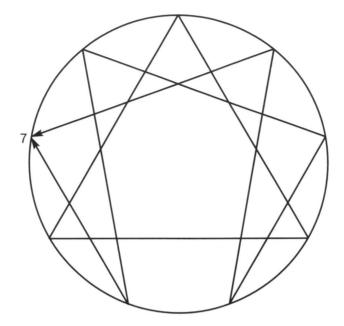

General Characterization of the Seventh Enneagram Point

The seventh Enneagram point represents the lower step of the reached goal. With this Enneagram point, you have reached the third and last segment of the Enneagram, which is characterized by the aimed-for goal. At the seventh Enneagram point, you can end your search—or you can continue the process—by going on to the eighth and ninth Enneagram points, and thus becoming completely absorbed in your goal.

PROCESSES

Processes

Finally, we have come to the goal; the process is where we have always wanted to have it.

1. Economic processes

At Enneagram Point 7, the circular course of the production process has been completed. Now what needs work is marketing and/or the organization of sales of the product.

2. Social processes

Finally we are living as we wish. In regard to groups, the conformity and the organization that lets the group live or work together productively has been found.

Personal Growth

At Point 7, you have reached the goal. You can look at yourself consciously and objectively. You have the ability to decide what you want. You are able to determine your future in such a way that you can get what you want. Here, the following important developmental stages have been reached:

1. You do not act unconsciously anymore.

2. You can keep up your clarity of consciousness over longer periods of time.

3. You no longer identify with your feelings and thoughts.

4. You have your own will.

That way, you have achieved what you wanted—to be master of your body, your feelings, and thoughts. But that does not mean that you do not suffer anymore. You can take on suffering voluntarily, but as a searching person, from that point on, you can live as you wish.

From this stage on, you have access to your higher centers. In order to be able to work with them, you must develop a special body. That means that you do not identify any longer with your different, antagonistic egos, but only observe the movements of your psyche, without interfering. Then you are able to react out of this detached attitude intuitively and securely. This ability to react securely from your higher centers corresponds in Tibetan Buddhism to the consciousness stage of the two highest chakras. On this level, the Buddhist texts emphasize, you are standing outside yourself—no longer identified with yourself—and you let your higher Self react. This attitude is what is meant by "the formation of a new body." Anyone who forms a new body is capable of waiting, and anyone who is able to have patience lays the foundation for acting out of his higher centers.

TYPE 7: THE OPTIMIST

Catch Words

The magical child (Eli Jaxon-Bear)

The versatile person (Richard Riso)

The epicurean (Helen Palmer)

The dreamer (Kathleen V. Hurley and Theodore E. Dobson)

The optimist (Klausbernd Vollmar)

The generalist

According to Ichazo: the greedy child

Key Words

The lowest step of the desired goal

Speed

Taking pleasure in making decisions

Superficial optimism

Doer/maker whose emphasis is on lust/desire

Idealist

According to Rohr and Ebert, the favorite sentence of type 7 is:

"I am happy."

For me, Type 7 is marked by the statement:

"Life is easy."

Or he may have even invented the sentence along with Type 3:

"Profundity is neurosis."

General Characterization

Type 7 is blessed with smashing optimism and quick perceptions. He is extremely active and acts fast. His entire life is characterized by a high speed which, though, does not bother him, since he loves speed. He can be called the most mobile type of the Enneagram.

The Optimist is highly sensitive to stimulation and has his hands in all kinds of affairs. He seldom commits himself and avoids pain and suffering wherever possible. By leaving all paths open for himself, he thinks he will be able to avoid suffering.

Type 7 is often greedy, and he wants to experience as much lust as possible. With Enneagram Point 7, we have entered the intellectual field of the Enneagram, shown at Point 7 in continuous investigations into all kinds of (often remote) fields of interest. The mobile intellect of Type 7 often dominates his emotions. Even though, at first sight, he may seem very emotional, he is rather rationally inclined.

The Optimist lives in the tension of

1. Unconcerned optimism and nervous activity

2. Versatility and depth.

Strength

Type 7 is the optimist of the Enneagram, radiating an engaging, childlike nature. He is the *puer aeternus* according to Carl Gustav Jung, and the female Type 7 is the *puella aeterna*. The seventh Enneagram type shows an astonishing lightness in social matters. He is unconcerned, funny, and a good entertainer. He is a child of luck (similar to Type 3), and due to his fast, perceptive faculty, he is intellectually facile, so he always had an easy time at school. In addition, he has multiple talents, and his interests reach in many directions.

Even though he is frequently inclined to be materialistic, Enneagram Type 7 has a strongly pronounced idealistic side. While he is funny, he is also a dynamic and ambitious human being, who always wants only the best.

The Optimist hates pain and avoids suffering whenever possible. That makes him seem agitated and driven.

Weakness (the Shadow)

Type 7 is frequently nervous, overly active, and much too fast, since he is constantly on the run from boredom and suffering. He searches everywhere for lust, which makes him into a pleasure-addicted dilettante or narcissist. Frequently, he is immoderate or even greedy, and his motto is "The more the better!" He especially loves new experiences. Through them, he represses the experience of pain and his fear of intimacy. Almost everyone of Type 7 is inclined toward the Don Juan syndrome (greed for sexual experience). He always thinks that he has to find an even better partner, quickly becoming bored with the old one.

EXERCISE: Decreasing Speed

The Optimist finds his calm and rest in going deeper. Quality instead of quantity is a healing maxim for him. The Enneagram Type 7 reaches depth by living much more slowly. He must force himself—at least at the beginning—to radically decrease his life speed, and at the same time he must stay with a thing or with a partner.

As a daily exercise, it helps the "racing" Type 7 to make Gurdjieff's demands his own: that you do everything that you do 100 per cent. Since Type 7 is, most of the time, finished with his work before the due date, he should force himself to use the remaining time to go over and deepen his work.

The Optimist must understand that the 100 percent completion of a task makes his life more important and gives him more depth. When he holds back and does not solve a task perfectly, he only hinders himself in reaching his goals, and from living 100 percent.

Type 7 needs daily meditation, for a quarter of an hour every evening—without fail. He should try not to identify himself with his thoughts and inner images. Even though he perceives them, he must not get stuck on them. It may help him to work with the affirmation:

"Thoughts come and go."

Meditation especially helps him to decrease his speed, to get to know himself better, and not to live solely at the surface.

Chakra

The throat chakra corresponds to the seventh Enneagram point. This chakra leads our communication, and Type 7 is often a brilliant master of communication. At the same time, seen from the order of the chakras and from the Enneagram, the spiritual here stands in the forefront. This is because, on a deep level, the throat chakra leads inward, since it is the one that asks the question of truth. Type 7 must ask himself this question, because as "jack of all trades," he storms through life, in the last analysis, on the run from himself.

EXERCISE: Inner Calm

It helps Enneagram Type 7 a lot to sit down calmly and mediate on his throat and his neck. He might then imagine that during calm and regular breathing, his throat becomes more and more relaxed and wider. He lets himself fall into this feeling deeper and deeper, and enjoys his inner calm.

Color

The color orange is allocated to this seventh Enneagram point. In this, the idealism of Type 7 is expressed, because traditionally the garments of Buddhist monks are colored orange, and orange is also the warm pole of the color spectrum, symbolizing sympathy. Type 7, who is often inclined to egocentricity, is thus reminded of his redemption, which lies in the attitude of compassion and warm-heartedness.

According to the second possibility of color allocation, the color yellow is allocated to this Enneagram point. This color allocation emphasizes the spiritual mobility of this Enneagram type.

Rohr and Ebert connect the color green with this Enneagram point, as the Jesuits do.

EXERCISE: The Color Orange

It helps the Optimist to, in deep relaxation, image the color orange in front of his inner eye. He concentrates on this with closed eyes, and holds the image for about ten breaths. Then he returns slowly to his everyday life.

COSMOLOGY

Astronomy

The seventh Enneagram point is brought into connection with the superpersonal planet Neptune, which rotates on the seventh planet orbit around the sun.

With the seventh Enneagram point, we have entered the spiritual and fine material area, which is expressed through the outer planets, which are not visible to the naked eye.

Astrology

As mentioned before, the planet Neptune corresponds to this Enneagram point, whose shadow symbolizes illusion. Illusion is a big problem for Enneagram Type 7, who easily fools himself in his superficiality. Type 7 always assumes that he is doing well, and that life is easy, no matter what happens. In the most difficult situations, he usually still cracks a joke. He is the sunny boy of the Enneagram, no matter how he is doing. Neptune draws his attention to this illusion but, at the same time, symbolizes the strength of the Optimist—being creative (like Type 4)—to the highest degree.

With Neptune, we enter the area of the superpersonal planets, and here again, it is necessary for this type to conquer the ego.

The sign of Capricorn is allocated to the seventh Enneagram point. As a sign that is dominated by Saturn, Capricorn calls for a necessary deepening for Type 7, which makes him healthier. As an earth sign, Capricorn emphasizes the necessity of grounding, which Type 7 forgets much too easily. Partially, the Capricorn principle can be seen as the exact counterimage to the Optimist. It shows precisely what this Enneagram point is lacking: Toughness, perseverance, and consciousness of problems. These characteristic features would help him keep from spending himself and running around in a neurotic way.

Animal Symbols

The symbol animal of the seventh Enneagram point is the monkey, who jumps just as restlessly from tree to tree as the interests of the Optimist jump around.

It is the same with the butterfly that flutters from one plant to the next.

Personalities

Typical representatives of Type 7 are darlings of the audience and forever optimists in film and on TV. Their philosophy was formed by the Greek philosopher Epicurus (341–271 B.C.), and especially by his pupil Aristippus, who claimed that the highest treasure of the human being is his lust and the highest evil his pain. Aristippus, as a typical Optimist, wanted to develop a life art that avoided any kind of pain. The pupils of Epicurus used to meet in a garden; above the entrance was supposedly written: "Here lust is the highest treasure."

Sir Lancelot, from the Arthur saga, could be called a Type 7. The Austrian composer Wolfgang Amadeus Mozart (1756–1791) was a complete and unequivocal Optimist. Walt Disney and Osho (Baghwna Sri Rajneesh) also belong to this group.

According to Freud, a neurotic has to be counted as Type 7, since he tries with great energy to ban any discomfort from his consciousness.

Country

Places allocated to the seventh Enneagram type are Ireland and Brazil. In both countries, the consciousness of poverty is displaced through the joy of living.

Astrology Neptune Capricorn
Color Orange
Chakra Vishuddha (throat chakra)
Kaballa Hod or partially for the dreamer aspect, also Daath (hidden Sephirot) Hod is powerful, scintillating, and brilliant, like the seventh Enneagram type, who can learn from Hod, to go philosophically into the depths that heal him, to act nobly, and to become sharp-witted.
Body Speaking tools
Bach blossoms Heather Water Violet
Feeling for Time Time is expandable, and one has the feeling that there is unlimited time for lust and fun. Type 7 often lives in the future, and flees from the present.

Key Questions

(The more questions you answer with yes,
the more pronounced is your resemblance
to Enneagram Type 7.)

1. Are you able to make connections quickly?

2. Do you think that life is basically easy?

3. Do you need your daily portion of excitement?

4. Are you experienced in many different fields, and have you had many different experiences?

5. Do you think of yourself as being capable of enthusiasm?

6. Do you see many possibilities for your future?

7. Would you agree with the sentence: "Profundity is neurosis"?

8. Do you avoid problems whenever you can?

9. Most of the time, do you have difficulty making decisions?

ENNEAGRAM POINT 8

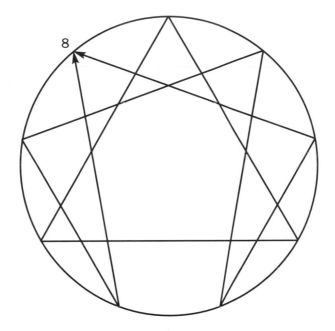

General Characterization of the Eighth Enneagram Point

With the eighth Enneagram point, you have already reached the highest step of your goal and of the Enneagram, because the ninth Enneagram point, in the last analysis, only represents a short transition to a new cycle. The eighth Enneagram ends the existing cycle.

At this Enneagram point, you have become completely absorbed in your goal. You can see this in the geometry of the Enneagram through the fact that the eighth Enneagram point is connected with the fifth and the second points. The fifth and the second Enneagram points both symbolize the highest stages of consciousness in their particular Enneagram sections (the second and first segments).

Processes

Processes

The process has not only reached its goal, but you have now become completely devoted to this process and are living it to perfection. You are, so to speak, absorbed in this process—or you might say that you serve this process.

1. Economic processes

The product is on the market. Its assets are perceived by the customers. Now it is necessary to direct everything towards the goal of satisfying the customer. This is so-called "customer service."

2. Social processes

Now you are completely absorbed in the group, with which you have gone through this process and you serve the group unselfishly. You know exactly what is good for the group, and act according to these principles without hesitation.

Personal Growth

On the level of the eighth Enneagram point, you have not only reached your goal, but you have also completely devoted yourself to it. You serve the life task that you have found here, and are satisfied—or you may perhaps be even beyond the level of satisfaction and dissatisfaction.

Spiritual leaders and wisdom teachers mostly stand at this Enneagram point, at which you could also place Gurdjieff and Ichazo.

EXERCISE: Affirmation

At this highest stage of the Enneagram, what is important is to give your best. You will progress here—and proceed to the transition point 9 at which you enter a new process—if you perform your work perfectly. Gurdjieff advised his students continually to do everything, whatever they did, 100 per cent, no matter what the cost. To perform a task 100 percent means to work in a highly concentrated and conscious way. In order to encourage yourself to do this kind of work, place a little card at your workplace on which you write:

"I take pleasure in performing my work perfectly."

You can also treat this sentence as an affirmation.

TYPE 8: THE BOSS

Catch Words

The warrior (Eli Jaxon-Bear)

The teacher (Richard Riso)

The boss (Helen Palmer, Klausbernd Vollmar)

The fighter (Kathleen V. Hurley and Theodore E. Dobson)

According to Oscar Ichazo: The mighty fighter for his ideals.

KEY WORDS

The perfection of the goal

Self-confidence

Security and strength

Aggression

The favorite sentence of Type 8, according to Rohr and Ebert:

"I am strong."

General Characterization

Type 8 is the most self-confident, but also the most self-righteous type in the Enneagram. According to the dynamics of the Enneagram, this type has not only reached his goal, but he is also completely absorbed it. The actions of the active "Boss" are formed by his ideas, to which he clings rigidly.

Enneagram Type 8 knows how to use circumstances to his own advantage at all times. His motto is "Divide and conquer." He is aggressive and acts with assurance.

Type 8 avoids weaker people, and therefore usually manipulates and controls others, but he can also act protectively.

He is capable of devotion and very dependent on possession.

He searches for justice and lives in the tension of

1. Self-righteousness, arrogance and social attitudes and views

2. Suppressed rage and open fight.

According to the original concept of the Enneagram, this type is a mediator, since he can not only look at situations (relatively) objectively, but since he also likes taking on a neutral attitude, which his great experience enables him to do.

Strength

The eighth Enneagram type is very fair and loves the truth. He has the strength to enforce justice. With his strong ability to assert himself, this Enneagram type is the ideal boss of a company. He does not act only as one who possesses power, but he can also mediate impartially in the name of justice.

With his enormous self confidence, he can be considered a model for many other Enneagram types.

Weakness (the Shadow)

Enneagram Type 8 tends to use others as objects for his goals and to dominate. He cannot tolerate limits, and therefore you almost never find him in subordinate positions.

He is often very aggressive when enforcing his goal; more sensitive types even impute to him that he sticks at nothing in order to enlarge his powerful position.

In sexuality, women of this type want total possession of their partner. Men demand complete devotion. Sexuality can easily become a game of power with Type 8.

EXERCISE: Perception

For the eighth Enneagram type it is important to really perceive the other person. For that reason, a perception exercise with a partner is useful. Type 8 should do it on a regular basis two or three times per week for about ten minutes.

Sit comfortably opposite a partner, relax, and then look directly into the eyes of the partner for about three minutes. Then close your eyes and try to visualize the image of the other person as precisely as possible. Visualize the image in detail for about two minutes and then open your eyes in order to compare the image in your mind with the one in front of you.

You can also do this exercise with a photograph.

With this exercise, you not only perceive the other person precisely, but you also recognize how quickly and unconsciously you project your own needs and views onto the other person. It helps the Enneagram Type 8 a lot to see that. With his self-righteousness and his ability to enforce things, he often does not really perceive other people at all.

Chakra

The Third Eye—also called Ajna chakra—is allocated to the Enneagram Type 8. The Third Eye symbolizes our spiritual forces, and the eighth Enneagram point stands centrally in the spiritual field of the Enneagram, according to Gurdjieff.

EXERCISE: Dissolving Tension

The eighth Enneagram type finds his relaxation by meditating on his Third Eye. He sits or lies down comfortably, closes his eyes and relaxes, as much as he can. In this deep relaxation, he sends a humming tone into his Third Eye. With a little practice, he can perceive this tone at the point of his Ajna chakra as a slightly tingly feeling. After about two to three minutes, he ends the humming and hears the humming tone in his Third Eye as an echo. After that, he ends the exercise.

Through this exercise, the tension, which is an expression of the materialistic, aggressive attitude of the Boss, will in the long run dissolve. This exercise, though, has to be done on a regular basis once a day for many months.

Color

The color orange is also allocated to the eighth Enneagram type, as it is to Type 7. This warmest of all colors reminds him of the fact that he has to service the universe (or God, if you want to see it that way). Orange is the color of the garments of the Buddhist monks who, sacrificing themselves, serve their ideals or their Higher Self.

With Enneagram Point 8, according to the opinion of Gurdjieff, the goal of a developmental process is achieved. This goal should always lead to something higher than a personal attitude. You could say that at Enneagram Point 8, you serve only the goal and nothing else. This is exactly what the orange-colored garments of the monks express. Here the ego was overcome.

According to the Jesuits, the colors black and white are allocated to the eighth Enneagram point. Black and white as colors that contain all other colors, characterize this Enneagram point well. As all light colors mix to white, all surface colors mix to black, which is called "the mother of colors." The black-white contrast presents the greatest possible color contrast, which symbolizes vividly the hardness of the eighth Enneagram point .

The meditation on the color orange, as described in detail in the chapter about the seventh Enneagram, can also help the Boss to show empathy and warmth. It is a challenge for him to accept these qualities, which are worthwhile for him.

COSMOLOGY

Astronomy

Uranus, the planet that was discovered at the start of the French Revolution, is allocated to the eighth Enneagram point. Uranus lies on the eighth and thus on the next to last orbit of the planets around the sun.

Astrology

With Uranus, we are in the superpersonal part of the Enneagram. Here higher or spiritual values are taking effect, now that the development through matter and feeling has come to an end. At the eighth Enneagram point, the human being can act consciously and can change his situation, an action that is also expressed by the Uranus principle. Uranus, as the octave of Mercury, expresses exquisitely the higher form of consciousness that is reached at Enneagram Point 8.

Pisces corresponds to the eighth Enneagram point. With the principle Pisces, the goal has been reached on the level of the zodiac. Pisces represents the twelfth and last sign of the zodiac—so to speak, its perfection.

The Pisces principle symbolizes the depth of the soul, which can be reached at the eighth Enneagram point. Female and male components come together here, because Pisces stands in different cultures as both male and female symbols. Thus, at Enneagram Point 8, the contrasts cancel each other out, and for a brief moment, time stands still in order then to enter—at the ninth Enneagram point—into a new cycle.

Animal Symbols

The type concepts of the Jesuits allocate such strong and dangerous animals as the rhinoceros, rattlesnake, tiger, and bull to the eighth Enneagram point.

Personalities

The classic Enneagram Type 8 was the Italian philosopher and politician Niccolo Macchiavelli (1469–1527), with his famous motto: "Right is whatever benefits the stronger person."

I also count George Ivanovitch Gurdjieff as well as the gestalt psychologist Fritz Perls to this Enneagram type. Both were considered very strong and at the same time cool personalities. To this category belong also the composer Ludwig van Beethoven (1770–1827) and Greek author Nikos Kazantzakis (1883–1957), who wrote among other books *Alexis Sorbas*, and the eccentric Madame Blavatsky, founder of the Theosophical Society. Henry Miller wrote as an author from the viewpoint of Type 8; as an actor, John Wayne played this type.

Country

Spain is the country that the Jesuits allocate to the eighth Enneagram point—the Spain that was admired by Type 8 Ernest Hemingway.

Astrology
Neptune
Saturn

Color
Orange

Chakra
Ajna chakra (Third Eye or Forehead chakra)

Kabbala
Jessod or partially also Chochma (Chokmah)
Jessod represents the real world to which the eighth Enneagram point eagerly turns. He can learn from Jessod how he inspires others and sensibly spurs them on.

Body
No allocation to body.

Bach blossoms
Vine
Chicory (blossoms of the relief type of the second Enneagram type)

Feeling of Time
Here you are absolutely on time. Type 8 has the feeling that he has to work constantly in favor of a better future.

Key Questions

(The more questions you answer with yes,
the more pronounced is your resemblance
to Enneagram Point 8.)

These questions that refer to Type 8 are based on the ideas of Ichazo

1. Do you have strong opinions, which you can hold well?

2. Are your actions formed by tactical considerations?

3. Do other people think that you are aggressive?

4. Is it easy for you to say no?

5. Do you tend to expose other people and to realize their weak points immediately?

6. Do you like strength in yourself and in others?

7. Do you have difficulties with superiors and authorities?

8. Do you consider yourself open and clear?

9. Is justice an important value for you?

Questions that refer to these types, according to the schools of the Fourth Way

1. Are you able to solve conflicts well?

2. Do people appreciate you because of your neutral attitude?

3. Do you like to fight?

ENNEAGRAM POINT 9

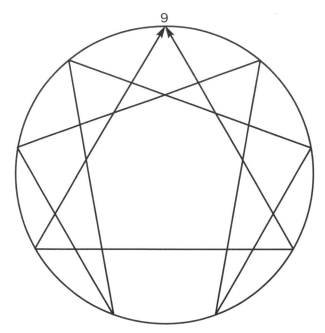

General Characterization of the ninth Enneagram point

Enneagram Point 9, as the last and third shock point of the Enneagram, holds a strange, ambiguous position. It shows, on one hand, the completion of a planned task; on the other hand, it stands for the transition to a new process. Therefore, this Enneagram point is called 0 as well as 9. You can see this situation clearly from its astrological position. It corresponds to Pluto as the planet farthest away from the Sun, while, at the same time, it corresponds to the sign of Aries, which marks the beginning of the zodiac.

Interestingly, we can also refer this Enneagram point—the beginning and end of a process—to the Tarot. As the end point of the development is the ninth card of the Major Arcana, the Hermit. He has realized who he really is and has had an important experience. The fool, to whom all possibilities are open, is a symbol of the Zero, from which everything is created, and indicates the beginning. If we look at the ninth Enneagram point as a goal to be reached, then Tarot card 21—the World—which indicates the highest personality development, corresponds to it too.

Processes

Processes

The ninth Enneagram point is the point of transition, which, in the system of the Enneagram, reminds us that life is never in a state of rest, but is a constantly rising movement.

Actually, it would be much clearer to imagine the Enneagram as an endless spiral, which completes one rotation in nine steps.

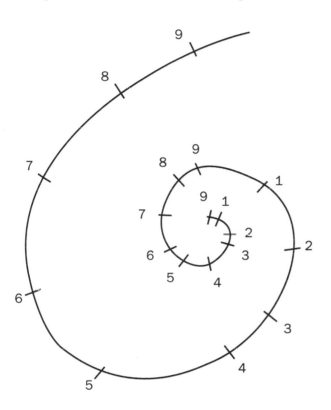

The Enneagram as Spiral II

In the illustration above we can see that the point 9 always leads to Point 1, and stands at the transition to a new process (a repeated turn of the spiral). At Enneagram Point 9, the process turns onto a new level. The understanding of this Enneagram point is essential to an understanding of the dynamics of the Enneagram.

Personal Growth

You have reached everything that you wanted to reach, and also a lot more—the existence of which you did not know at the beginning of your path. Here, the question is whether you want to remain in this state or enter a new process on a higher level, because of the experiences you have had, and run through the nine points of the Enneagram all over again.

The Enneagram represents itself as a symbol of life processes. At the three shock points, something specific happens—you find a teacher, for example, or a drastic event takes place—and before you can turn around, you are on another level of consciousness, which can often seem like living in another world. Here, at the third shock point—Enneagram Point 9—you can create a transition into another world, into a new way of vision, or behavior. That means you can make the transition into the new level of consciousness consciously—not mechanically.

Nine is the number of the goal to be reached. In the art of fortune-telling, it indicates the lucky/happy completion of a process.

C. G. Jung tells of a treasure that blooms every nine months and nine years. If it is not found on the last night, it sinks down into the earth, and everything begins again.[23] The treasure is the gold of the soul that we are capable of lifting through the nine steps of the Enneagram. Anyone who misses the right point in time must begin again from the beginning. Gurdjieff emphasizes this idea in regard to the shock points, and especially in regard to the third shock point: The right point in time is essential.

123

Economic Processes

At this point, you can think about whether you want to produce a follow-up product or add another product or service to those you offer now. If that is the case, you will enter the circular course of the Enneagram again, on a new level.

Social Processes

Either you remain on the level of the eighth Enneagram point, or you can turn to a new and extended task on the level of the ninth Enneagram point.

TYPE 9: THE LOVER

Catch Words

The saint (Eli Jaxon Bear)

The peace-lover (Richard Riso)

The mediator (Helen Palmer)

The keeper/preserver (Kathleen V. Hurley and Theodore E. Dobson)

The lover (Klausbernd Vollmar)

According to Oscar Ichazo: the lazy genius.

Key Words

The point of the transition

Peace-loving

Harmonious

Phlegmatic, lazy, idle

Passive

According to Rohr and Ebert, this type lives according to the motto:

"I am satisfied/content."

Frequently, you may hear Type 9 say:

"We want to get along again. Everything is only half as bad as it seems."

General Characterization

The ninth and last Enneagram type is the most peaceful and at the same time the laziest type of the entire Enneagram. He is often very passive and dependent on a harmonious atmosphere. Under all circumstances, he avoids conflicts. His striving is for union, and he has understood that the high ideal of love, which represents an open attitude, is marked by empathy and solidarity. But often, at first, he seeks tranquility. A part of him, deep down in his heart, is a typical householder who lives by the motto:

"I want to have peace and quiet."

If this peace is disturbed, Type 9 can become astonishingly cranky, stubborn, and unpleasant. Despite all his striving for harmony and peacefulness, he knows how to assert himself.

On the other hand, the Lover has excellent insight into human nature, and people therefore often ask his advice. People simply feel understood by him; he seems to be sending out healing forces.

He patiently takes his time, gives encouragement and advice and always conveys harmony.

The Lover himself lives in the tension of:

1. peacefulness and fight

2. insight and lazy indecision.

Strength

Enneagram Type 9 is immensely sociable and astonishingly peaceable. He can spread a field of harmony around himself, and he can help others to get into the same kind of harmonious state. He uses his insight into others without any ulterior motives or tendency to manipulation. The ideal profession for the ninth Enneagram type is that of a therapist. He could also be a diplomat, especially since this type can hold back his own ego and its problems.

Enneagram Type 9 has no problems with sexual identity. If he is sometimes inclined to live his sexuality at random, it will probably turn out well for him and for his partners most of the time.

Weakness (the Shadow)

Enneagram Type 9 is extremely lazy and often idle. Frequently, he lacks interest in anything; he is without motivation and phlegmatic and cannot be bothered to do anything. In addition, his gentle manner, which often seems put on, can make many other Enneagram types furious. The Lover often has a very boring effect on Type 3, 4, and 7—and yes, indeed, sometimes they don't take him seriously.

The ninth Enneagram type shows such passive behavior because he cannot tolerate conflict. To achieve harmony, he often sweeps a lot of things under the rug that should actually be on the table! But Enneagram Type 9 does not address problems well (only developed Lovers like C. G. Jung, who are helped by their sympathetic understanding, succeed in that).

In this type, it is not surprising that indirect resistance comes up when he is threatened and attacks are made on his peace. In such situations, Type 9 becomes extremely stubborn, resists his opponent, and defies him with such passive intensity that every attack comes to a dead end in time. I would say that the Lover is a master of passive aggression and indirect resistance, which causes every opponent to despair.

EXERCISE: Dreamwork and the Shadow

I think it is very important for Type 9 to express his aggressiveness openly and directly. He must understand that his shadow is always his aggressiveness, and it belongs to the entirety of his personality and must be integrated. Only then can Type 9 really live out his need for harmony. Here, we find many individuals who are involved in combative sports, such as judo, karate, and aikido .

I would also suggest to the Lover to analyze his dreams regularly and pay attention to what haunts, attacks, and bothers him. That is his shadow, which wants to be taken in by him, and which he should look at more carefully. It might help to paint it.

In addition, aggression exercises from bioenergetics may help him, but he should perform them in a group with a qualified instructor.

Chakra

The highest chakra of the human being—the crown or Sahasrara chakra, which is also called the thousand-petaled lotus—corresponds to the last Enneagram point.

Just as, at Enneagram Point 9, a process is brought to its end and a new process is announced, so the seventh human chakra marks a transition—or return point. Here, the highest consciousness and the highest clarity is reached, in order to allow the energies to fall down again into the coarse, physical area. Enneagram Point 9, just like the Sahasrara chakra, must under no circumstances be misunderstood as a resting place. Rather, it forms the transition to a new level, which in human life means looking at oneself and at one's environment with a new level of consciousness. You have become more conscious of yourself with your shadow side and strengths, with your projections and intuitions, and you deepen this consciousness even further by running through the new cycle again. That is what the thousand-petaled lotus and the ninth Enneagram Point indicate to us—transition points in the system.

You get up to the forehead chakra at Enneagram Point 8 with the help of a teacher and with special techniques, but you only reach the crown chakra when you don't automatically stick with any precepts that come from the past or from others anymore. At this point, you have become a grown-up. You independently reach the highest state of consciousness. Gurdjieff says that the highest goal of a human being is to become an individual. Exactly that is expressed in Yogic philosophy by the step toward the conscious stage of the crown chakra.

127

Color

It is logical that the color red is allocated to Type 9, the enhancement or completion of the Enneagram. In Goethe's color circle, red represents the enhancement of the two primary colors yellow and blue. Red, according to Goethe, or purple, is the king of colors, which is why kings used to wear garments of this color.

Red symbolizes blood and fire and thus human passion, which pulls this Enneagram type out of his laziness with enormous energy. Lovers therefore should pay special attention to this color, because red inspires energy and activity.

Whether they paint red pictures or visualize themselves as red people (wrapped in a red cloud) does not matter. What is important is their concentration on red energy.

COSMOLOGY

Astronomy

The ninth orbit of the planets is occupied by Pluto, the planet that is furthest away from the solar system.

Pluto symbolizes an incomprehensible, fine material energy, but one that can become highly explosive. After all, Pluto was discovered at the same time that the first nuclear fission came to the laboratory.

With Pluto, for the time being, the circle of the planets closes, just as with Enneagram Point 9, the Enneagram has, for the time being, completed itself.

Astrology

Just as the rainbow begins with the color red, so does the zodiac begin with the energy of Aries, which is also connected with the color red and the ninth Enneagram point. Here, the energy of the beginning is emphasized; it is inherent in this last Enneagram point, according to Gurdjieff, Ouspensky, and Bennett.

The ninth Enneagram point characterizes the end and the beginning of a process. You could also say that it represents two different perspectives on a transition. That is also expressed in its astrological allocation to Pluto and Aries, because Pluto represents the octave of Mars, which rules the sign of Aries. When the highest energy form has been reached (the octave), we must turn again to a lower form of energy. After a greater consciousness has been reached, we must work at integrating this new state. As is so well stated:

> "Before the enlightenment: Fetching water and chopping wood; after the enlightenment: Fetching water and chopping wood."

Animal Symbols

Peace-loving animals are allocated to this Enneagram point: The elephant as a good-natured animal, which is usually considered thick-skinned and easy-going; the whale, which represents the water animal, similar in character to the elephant, and especially the dolphin, as an extremely peaceful and social animal.

Personalities

The two important psychotherapists, Carl Gustav Jung and Carl Rogers, also the American myth researcher Joseph Campbell, who was influenced by Jung, and the German physicist Albert Einstein, who actively worked for peace, belong to the Lover group.

The Jesuits regard the Indian guru Ramana Maharshi and the English poet Ezra Pound as very developed representatives of this type.

Country

Mexico is considered the classical country for Type 9—at least, as seen from the U.S. point of view.

Astrology Pluto Aries
Color Red (purple)
Chakra Sahasrara (crown chakra)
Kabbala Schechina or Kether Schechina emphasizes the sympathizing, peaceable side of the ninth Enneagram type. It spurs him on to mysticism. Kether, as crown, and Schechina as divine wisdom, emphasize that from Gurdjieff's point of view, this is the highest and most developed of all the Enneagram types.
Body Brain (cortex)
Bach Blossoms Wild Rose Oak (as the blossom of the relief type of the third Enneagram point)
Feeling for Time Time is a matter of the moment. Yet, in stress, Type 9 either adheres rigidly to time-related plans, or is notoriously late and often forgets his appointments. Frequently, Type 9 has the feeling that other people demand too much time from him and thus take energy away from him. On the other hand, Type 9 can simply let time go by and do nothing. He would prefer to hold onto the past, since he feels comfortable in it.

130

Key Questions

(The more questions you answer with yes,
the more pronounced is your resemblance
to Enneagram Type 9.)

1. Do you often make things as comfortable as possible for yourself?

2. Do you consider sympathy and solidarity to be essential virtues?

3. Are you able to turn off your mind successfully?

4. Do you get along well with others?

5. Do other people think of you as a "lame duck"?

6. When it comes to tasks, do you often procrastinate?

7. Do you often catch yourself not paying attention to what you are doing?

8. Are you inclined to avoid making decisions?

9. Do you do everything you can to achieve a peaceful atmosphere?

6. The Dynamics of the Model

This chapter describes the combination possibilities of the individual Enneagram qualities, revealing the complexity and dynamics of this model.

Movement Directions in the Enneagram

In the equilateral triangle and in the hexagon of the Enneagram, two different directions are possible. I call them

1. the stress direction

2. the relief direction

1. The stress direction is determined by the following path through the Enneagram:

a) in the Hexagon:
$1 \rightarrow 4; 2 \rightarrow 8; 4 \rightarrow 2; 5 \rightarrow 7; 7 \rightarrow 1;$
and $8 \rightarrow 5$

b) in the triangle:
$3 \rightarrow 9; 6 \rightarrow 3;$ and $9 \rightarrow 6$

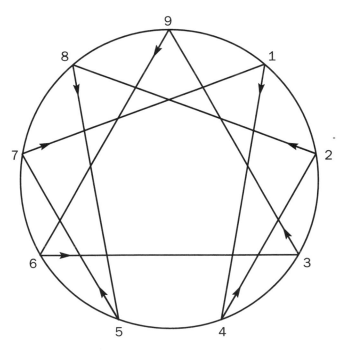

The stress direction in the Enneagram

2. The relief direction is determined by the following path through the Enneagram:

a) in the Hexagon:
   $1 \rightarrow 7$; $2 \rightarrow 4$; $4 \rightarrow 1$; $5 \rightarrow 8$; $7 \rightarrow 5$; and $8 \rightarrow 2$,

b) in the triangle:
   $3 \rightarrow 6$; $6 \rightarrow 9$; and $9 \rightarrow 3$

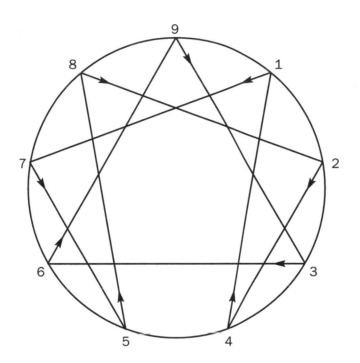

The relief direction in the Enneagram

In a stress situation, a human being usually reacts according to the defense mechanisms of his own type. When the stress increases, he usually reacts according to the so-called stress point of his type. This will clarify the Enneagram strategies you see in conflicts.

Rohr and Ebert[24] base their considerations on the fact that stressed people usually try to get consolation from their stress types. This consolation, of course, turns out to be deceptive and often leads even deeper into inner tension.

Riso[25] even claims that a movement toward the stress types leads inevitably to neurosis and illness.

In times of mental balance, a human being is inclined to live the positive sides of his own type. If this mental balance lasts for a long time period, he will react according to his relief type. Anyone who, in the long run, makes the reactions of the relief type his own, will get healthy and can live himself.

Stress Points as Shadow Projections

It seems to me that the stress points express the shadow of each type.

In Type 1, who must always be right, for example, lives a refusing Type 4, who thinks that he is something special and is extremely vulnerable.

In Type 2, who serves others in order to manipulate them, lives a latent Type 8, who asserts himself harshly toward others when it matters.

In every performance-oriented Type 3 lives a repressed, lazy type 9, just as in every sensitive Type 4, an unnoticed Type 2 resides, who serves others and is thus able to hold back his ego.

In the profound Type 5 lives an unaccepted, flaky Type 7, and in the gullible civil servant Type 6, an extremely work-friendly Type 3 makes himself noticeable as a shadow projection.

The superficial Type 7 projects his shadow onto the obstinate Type 1.

The elbowing-type 8 cannot bear the indecisive and passive Type 5.

And the lazy Type 9 rejects the civil servant in himself, which Type 6 symbolizes.

These shadow projections show why we react in stress situations in a way that we cannot stand! Here we clearly show our shadow side.

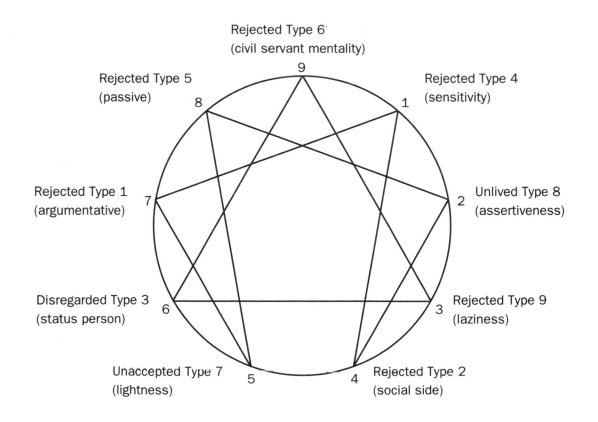

Shadow Projections in the Enneagram

Stress Points and the Choice of Partner

Point	Stress Point	Stress Point of Stress Point	Relief Point
1	4	2	7
2	8	5	8
3	9	6	3
4	2	8	1
5	7	1	8
6	3	9	9
7	1	4	5
8	5	7	2
9	6	3	3

When we choose a partner who personifies our stress type, we are able to learn a lot together, but the learning process is extremely difficult. If we have, on the other hand, chosen a partner who corresponds to our relief type, then we get along very well most of the time and we can rest together and relax.

Since, in the last analysis, nobody personifies a pure Enneagram type in all situations, the picture becomes even more complex with the choice of a partner. All the different types in one person communicate with all the different types in the partner. Let's examine this model—not as a bible for the choice of the suitable partner, but as a guide to how we can better understand partner conflicts.

I have observed, for example, that the stress point of the type that is the stress point to my type often baffles me completely. For example, I am a 7 and my stress point is Type 1. The stress point of Type 1 is Type 4, and Type 4 baffles me.

Similarly, the strict Type 1 tends to misunderstand the serving Type 2.

The Type 2, so keyed to others, misunderstands the withdrawn Type 5.

The Type 3 can't figure out the vulnerable Type 6.

The sensitive Type 4 doesn't grasp the ways of the loud Type 8.

The reserved Type 5 misunderstands the moralizing Type 1.

The vulnerable Type 6 doesn't comprehend the harmony-seeking Type 9.

The often superficial Type 7 misinterprets the profound Type 4.

The power-obsessed Type 8 cannot comprehend the indolent Type 7.

And the lazy Type 9 is baffled by the workaholic Type 3.

When judging partners, it is a good idea to observe the following points:

1. The Enneagram is divided up differently by Gurdjieff than by Ichazo.

According to Gurdjieff:

1	2	3
4	5	6
7	8	9

According to Ichazo:

9	1	2
3	4	5
6	7	8

Partners who belong to the same Enneagram segment often spontaneously find a common basis of understanding.

2. Examine the relationship of the relief points of both partners.

If the relief point of one partner is the stress point of the other, misunderstandings will only too easily take place in the relationship. If you are in an Enneagram position that your partner cannot understand from his stress point position, there will be permanent misunderstandings. You will interpret the behavior of your partner incorrectly, since he is incomprehensible to you.

The following descriptions point out what happens in tense situations. When you see through your tendencies to mechanical reactions, you can also work at reducing them.

STRESS POINT 1 → 4

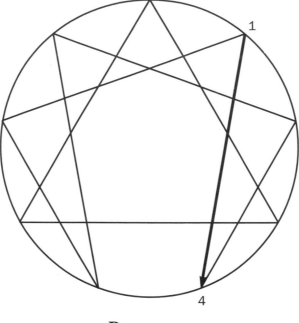

Processes

Line of sight in processes

The line of sight from the first Enneagram point to the fourth combines two different fields.

At Enneagram Point 1, we are looking at the material and basic pre-conditions of a process, while at the fourth Enneagram point, it is necessary to overcome Type 4's typical resistance to a process, and to better understand the course the process must take. The resistances and crises that unavoidably occur at Enneagram Point 4 can easily lead to a discontinuance of the process. This can be avoided, though, by clearly realizing the possible difficulties from the beginning. When you know where in the process the discouraging Enneagram Point 4 could emerge, the crisis can be overcome faster and better. The line of sight from the first to the fourth Enneagram point helps us:

1. deal with the crisis and not repress our reactions so that we react too late

2. search for the cause of the crisis in our pre-conditions.

At this line of sight in the Enneagram, we can get out of the way of the danger of experiencing the eternal loop of a process. This loop would have us ogling the crisis situation at Enneagram Point 4 and moving back to earlier stages of the process. Here it is easy to fall back to the first or second Enneagram point. We long for the less problematic situation of the past. This fall-back can be avoided by considering from the beginning the crisis that will come at Enneagram Point 4, and thus helping the process to take a speedy course.

136

THE STRESSED ENTREPRENEUR

Key Words

Crestfallen to depressed person

Self-destructive critic

Moody contemporary, in case of economic failures.

Characterization of this combination

Psychology

What comes from Type 1	What comes from Type 4
Eager striving to be perfect and complete, especially in material fields	Feeling of being something special
The expression of repressed rage and aggression through the inclination to:	The expression of rage and aggression through:
1. nitpicky criticism 2. considering one's own opinion to be the only correct one	1. aggression 2. moody behavior

Result

The first Enneagram type thinks of himself as always being right, and he can only with difficulty tolerate it when other people have an opinion that he doesn't approve of. In addition, he eagerly strives for perfection and completion, especially in money matters, which can easily cause stress for him. If something goes wrong, he turns into a critic who is barely tolerable.

In everyday life, this Enneagram type must suppress a lot of rage, which is asleep in him and expressed by his inclination to criticize and deliver moral tirades. If under stress he turns toward Type 4 and becomes easily depressed and self-destructive, turning his rage against himself. He is then often unbearably moody and under pressure to represent something special.

137

STRESS POINT 2 → 8

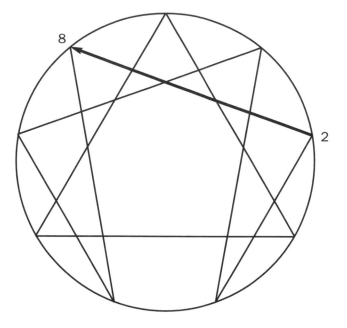

Processes

Line of sight in processes

When we look from the second toward the eighth Enneagram point, we see the goal of the process. It becomes clear where the goal lies. For this precise goal, determination is necessary in order to:

1. build up energy for the completion of the process

2. organize all our efforts toward the achievement of the goal

3. be able to analyze each step of the process to see whether it brings us closer to the desired goal.

At Enneagram Point 2, there is often the feeling that the process will get going only with the utmost difficulty, but if the goal of the process is clearly in front of our eyes, we will overcome these beginning difficulties more easily.

THE STRESSED PLANNER

Key Words

Open aggression

Blind destruction of affection and love

Characterization of this combination

Psychology

What comes from Type 2	What comes from Type 8
Manipulation through aesthetics and flattery	Direct expression of aggression
Unexpressed rage and aggression	Showing of strength
	Ability to assert oneself

Result

When Type 2 comes under stress—for example, when his aesthetic creation is not being acknowledged and he does not have the power to create a beautiful atmosphere—the actually good-natured Type 2 suddenly becomes frighteningly aggressive. He then tries to assert himself by approaching Enneagram Type 8, with elbows outspread, with open aggression and without any consideration for losses. At first, though, most of the time he reveals a rather passive aggression, which poisons the atmosphere. If that does not bring him to his goal, then he is even capable, in extreme cases, of becoming violent. These ways of behaving bring Type 2 into even greater stress, since now he has destroyed all the affection that he wanted to earn and which he actually had earned. He is often left at the end completely unloved and also powerless.

STRESS POINT 4 → 2

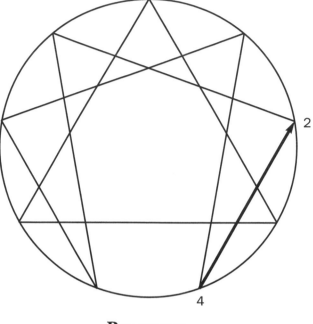

Processes

Line of sight in processes

The line of sight from the fourth to the second Enneagram point represents the most dangerous line of sight in the Enneagram. From the experience of the crisis at Enneagram Point 4, one looks back with a wistful glance at the earlier situation, which seemed to be much easier, where there were no such harsh frustrations and where the process seemed to begin to roll. This backward glance is seductive, causing us to fall back and to fail again and again at the same spot. You can observe this mechanism very well in relationships: If you do not go beyond the fourth Enneagram point, the point of the greatest frustration, you will fail in every relationship that follows at exactly this point, and will never proceed. What can be so clearly experienced in relationships can also be applied to any kind of process.

This line of sight in the Enneagram is only productive when you realize that the second Enneagram point does not represent an option anymore—not when you're already at Point 4.

THE STRESSED AFFLICTED PERSON

Key Words

The attempt to get love through serving

Self-aggression, since Type 4 has not learned to really associate with others.

Deterrent self-pity.

Characterization of this combination

Psychology

What comes from Type 4	**What comes from Type 2**
Feeling like something special and therefore having difficulties entering into genuine relationships with others	Making oneself indispensable
Self-aggression	The attempt to get love through manipulation

Result

When Enneagram Type 4 gets into stress situations—which can happen quickly with him—at first he becomes even more moody and unpredictable. If this stress lasts, then he tries in his distress, to get the affection of others through service. Most of the time he makes himself indispensable to his partner or his company. With his attitude of being something special, however, he reaches his limits, since it is important for him to take a popular stance or a "normal" one.

In addition, it is hard for Type 4 to enter a genuine relationship. The service turns into passive aggression, and he quickly begins to hate those whom he serves. He ends up completely unhappy and unloved in unbearable self-pity.

STRESS POINT 5 → 7

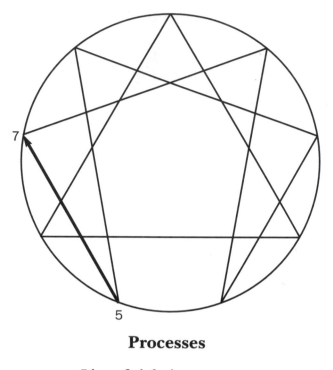

Processes

Line of sight in processes

Most of the time, at the fifth Enneagram point, one suffers from the fact that the goal has not yet been reached. Now it is important not to lose sight of the vision of the goal, as it will represent itself at Enneagram Point 7. One needs to take the vision as a stimulus and orient all one's efforts completely toward that goal, no matter what the cost.

THE STRESSED OBSERVER

Key Words

Sense crisis

Nervous aimless activity

Betrayal of his strength, his profundity

Characterization of this combination

Psychology

What comes from Type 5	What comes from Type 7
Retreat	Nervous activity
The inclination to deny all values	Search for lust

Result

Under stress, Enneagram Point 5 reacts desperately. He no longer sees any sense in life, and he retreats even further into himself. If the burden becomes even bigger, he turns to the behavior of Type 7, which is not suitable for him, since he doesn't have the lightness and superficiality of Type 7. So, Type 5 finds himself in nervous, aimless activity, and he does not find the lust that he is searching for. He becomes more and more eccentric and superficial, and with that, he betrays his strength—his profound qualities.

STRESS POINT 7 → 1

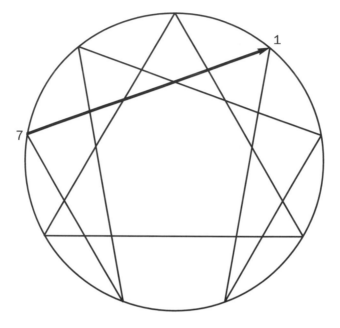

Processes

Line of sight in processes

At Point 7 you have reached the first step of your goal and now it is important to think about whether you want to continue in the process or remain at this point for the time being. In order to decide, it is helpful to glance back at the first Enneagram point. It makes clear how everything began and what the pre-conditions were when you plunged into this process. It was at this place that you first visualized the goal, which you have now reached. At that time you had only a limited concept of the path you were going to take.

Today, probably, you would see your path differently.

If you remember that and keep it in mind, you will be able to decide whether to proceed to Enneagram Point 8 and 9 in order to complete the process, or whether you are content with the stage you have already reached.

Furthermore, the line of sight from the seventh to the first Enneagram point often suggests that you enter on the next level into a new process. With the experiences you've had now, you can do it.

THE STRESSED OPTIMIST

Key Words

Radical activity on the flight from suffering

Rationalizing your own path and your own view of the world

Fighting off all other opinions

Characterization of this combination

Psychology

What comes from Type 7	**What comes from Type 1**
Lots of activity, with an emphasis on lust	Rationalizing one's own actions through a perfect system
	Criticizing of all other opinions

Result

Stress has an activating effect on Type 7—at first. The Optimist begins to act even more and to turn even more to different fields, from which he expects to find lust. But through this, most of the time, the pressure becomes greater. In this danger and distress, Type 7 turns from the flight from suffering to the strategies of Type 1. The Entrepreneur strives for perfection and rationalizes his view of the world and his way of living with a perfect system, which gives him security. The stressed Type 7 now tries that method, behaving in an intolerant way towards the outside, and thus he loses his lightness. He harshly criticizes anyone who does not agree with his opinions and ridicules them, until at the end, Type 7 is left standing completely alone.

145

STRESS POINT 8 → 5

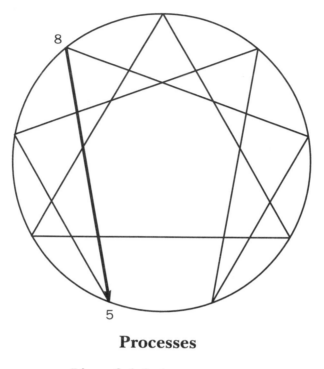

Processes

Line of sight in processes

At the eighth Enneagram point, the searcher has devoted himself completely to this task and/or to his goal. Only when he looks back from this situation to the fifth Enneagram point, is it clear to him what he has achieved. It is especially important for him that he is no longer being ruled by his feelings anymore, as he was at the fifth Enneagram point. At the eighth Enneagram point, he is the master of his feelings, without having to repress them.

Furthermore, this line of sight refers to the fact he could, especially in regard to his feelings, begin a new process again, and thus could surrender himself anew to the experience of the nine Enneagram points. On the other hand, the searcher may rest for the time being (Gurdjieff, though, would warn you not to rest too long, because he was of the opinion that you may never stop working consciously for more than eight hours).

THE STRESSED BOSS

Key Words

Great aggressiveness

Demoralizing brooding

Complete retreat into himself

Characterization of this combination

Psychology

What comes from Type 8	What comes from Type 5
Aggressiveness	The thinking that becomes brooding
	The tendency to retreat
	The tendency to self-doubt

Result

If Enneagram Type 8 comes into a stress situation, he reacts with frightening violence and aggression. But this behavior brings him even more stress, so he changes his behavior and turns to the characteristics of Enneagram Type 5. Under the influence of this Enneagram type, he begins to ponder and think about the world, which often puts him into a depression. This brooding often leads Type 8 to reproach himself and his environment in the strongest way. He ends up completely withdrawn, lost in thought and desperate.

147

STRESS POINT 9 → 6

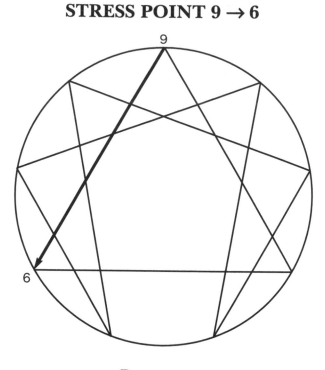

Processes

Line of sight in processes

This line of sight from the ninth to the sixth Enneagram point is always characterized by the fact that you are entering into a new process and looking for the impulses from the outside that could set the new process in motion. At this point, the searching person knows that he needs a new conscious impulse (the second shock point is the conscious one) in order to proceed.

Here, the dynamics of the Enneagram are revealed in a special sense—through the fact that the desired Enneagram Point 6 can emerge at Enneagram Point 9 and thus give the movement impulse it needs so that it can continue. That is to say, on a higher level of the Enneagram, you can imagine the three shock points as being mobile, and what really matters is how you characterize them.

THE STRESSED LOVER

Key Words

Extreme passivity

Search for security

Complete surrender of any kind of independence

Complete surrender of any kind of awake consciousness

Characterization of this combination

Psychology

What comes from Type 9

Laziness and passivity

What comes from Type 6

Thinking about security (which shows in its liberated form as playful dealing with situations and things)

Making oneself dependent on others as the Shadow of their independence

Unconsciousness (the sleep, according to Gurdjieff)

Result

Under stress, Type 9 can become more and more passive, idle, and astonishingly lazy. If the stress increases even more, then it urges him to search for security, which he often finds in the security-oriented thinking of Type 6. Most of the time, the result is that Type 9 makes himself more and more dependent on other people and institutions and does not think for himself anymore at all—living as in a sleep. He ends up in exactly that attitude that Gurdjieff condemns so much: being completely mechanically guided from outside, forgetting himself, and constantly sleeping.

149

STRESS POINT 3 → 9

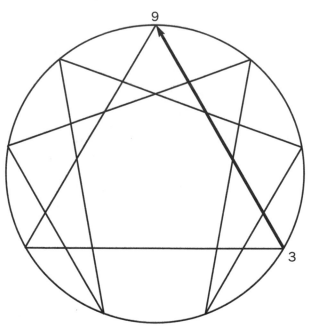

Processes

Line of sight in processes

At Enneagram Point 3, it takes all of one's imagination and powers of visualization to comprehend the ninth Enneagram point. This ninth Enneagram point, which at the same time represents the completion of the process and the transition to a new process, symbolizes only a fleeting state.

The glance from the third to the ninth Enneagram point can show us point by point the entire dynamics of the Enneagram, at which all the Enneagram points are seen as one. At the unconscious shock point (Enneagram Point 3), the role of the consciousness (Enneagram Point 9) becomes clear, as does the eternal movement of the Enneagram.

Referred concretely and directly to the practical process, this line of sight brings few impulses.

THE STRESSED MAGICIAN

Key Words

Hard work

Passivity

Self aggression up to suicide

Characterization of this combination

Psychology

What comes from Type 3	What comes from Type 9
Hard work	Passivity
Dependence on image	Self-aggression

Result

Type 3—for whom, as Magician, self-representation is more important than anything else—reacts under stress with even more mobilization of labor, and at the same time, he tries to get the upper hand again with deceit and fraud. He attempts to manipulate the situation as cleverly as possible. But if he does not succeed in doing so, he turns to the behavior of Type 9. Astonishingly, he does not do anything anymore, and goes completely passive, moving with bitterness through life. But this attitude can suddenly change again, when recognition still does not take place. Then he turns all his aggressiveness, with which he formerly brought down his competitors, against himself. These tactics, which are known to be Type 9's, can, according to Rohr and Ebert, lead to suicide. The "eternal sleep" is seen as the only way out of the image crisis.

STRESS POINT 6 → 3

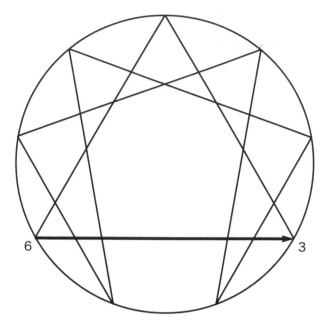

Processes

Line of sight in processes

Here, the searching person looks from the conscious to the unconscious shock point. It becomes clear to him that an outside impulse alone is not enough to bring the process to its happy end. At this point, it becomes clear that he must deal with an outside impulse consciously, actively, and attentively, in order to be able to use it for moving on.

THE STRESSED HERO

Key Words

Distrust and authoritative behavior

Compensation of stress through work

Sadism

Characterization of this combination

Psychology

What comes from Type 6	What comes from Type 3
Authoritative behavior and steadfast purpose	Workaholism
Distrust	Use of deceit and fraud

Result

Especially under stress, Type 6 becomes unbearably presumptuous, authoritarian, and distrustful, which makes life seem to him even more difficult. If stress increases, the Hero of Type 6 tries to save himself through an abundance of work, and strives with all his power and with all his means for success. But despite his knowledge, he lacks the mobility for that, and also the organizational talents of Type 3, so that he fails in this attitude. That makes him even more authoritarian, and in rare cases, causes him to become sadistic.

RELIEF POINTS

Relief points do not necessarily have to be connected with positive feelings. Gurdjieff worked mainly with the stress points, since this is where tension in the person is clearest and he can become conscious of his false personality. The problem with the relief points lies in the fact that when we are relaxed, only a little consciousness shows up. There, where we are doing well, we are unfortunately not very conscious. On the other hand, we can at these points be very relaxed, and that has a healing effect.

The following descriptions show how the types react in relaxed situations. They may help you to experience your mechanical reactions more consciously, and they can reveal ways of behaving with which you can stabilize yourself.

RELIEF POINT 1 → 7

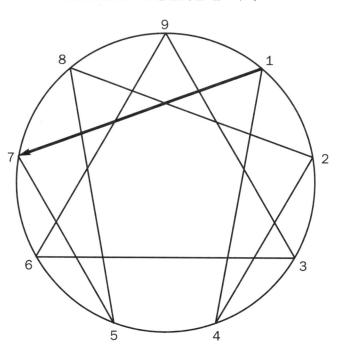

Processes

Line of sight in processes

If you look from the first Enneagram point to the seventh, you will visualize your goal. This line of sight is necessary because, without it, a process would never get into motion at all. From the tension between what is and what could be, one wins the motivation and the energy to enter into a development process. At the beginning of the Enneagram, you look at your pre-conditions in view of your goal, which—even though it is far in the distance—at first determines your further path. You use the goal like a guidepost that shows you where you have to go.

From this line of sight, the advice of the Sufis has to be understood (Abd al-Khaliq Gudschduwani defined in as early as the llth century):

"Keep your attention constantly before your eyes at every step."

154

THE RELAXED ENTREPRENEUR

Key Words

Rigidity is being loosened.

Rigidity and perfection are replaced by indolence and pleasure.

Characterization of this combination

Psychology

What comes from Type 1	What comes from Type 7
Rigidity and inflexibility	Indolence
Strictness	Optimism
Perfection	Enjoyment of life

Result

The first Enneagram type, who often goes through life tensely, rigidly, and in a controlled way, finds his relaxation by turning to the indolent behavior of Type 7, who makes life amusing for himself, is loosened up, and is a great optimist. These are all healing attitudes for Type 1, who is always in danger of turning into a strict, dogmatic perfectionist or into a rigid materialist. The behaviors of Type 7 loosen up Type 1 and help him to become cheerful and able to enjoy life in a relaxed way.

RELIEF POINT 2 → 4

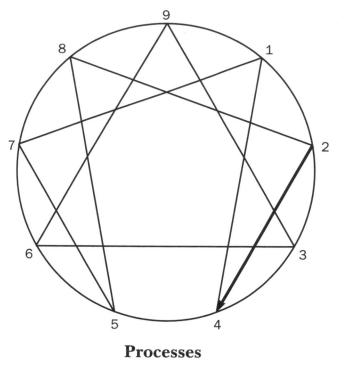

Processes

Line of sight in processes

The glance from the second Enneagram point to the fourth is characterized by a realism that is necessary in order to continue in the process. At the second Enneagram point, the task became clear to the searching person, and the glance towards the fourth Enneagram point shows him that this task cannot be fulfilled without inner struggle, tensions, and crises. This insight allows him to prepare for difficulties, so that they can be dealt with more easily. The situation corresponds to the point of sight from the first to the fourth Enneagram point. The only difference lies in the fact that at Enneagram Point 2, you can recognize your task and see your pre-conditions more clearly.

THE RELAXED PLANNER

Key Words

From the orientation toward others to the consciousness of one's self

Instead of dependency, the ability to live one's own life

More realistic self-image

Characterization of this combination

Psychology

What comes from Type 2	**What comes from Type 4**
The attempt to make others dependent on him	Paying attention to oneself
Easily becoming dependent himself	Living independently
Making himself indispensable	a positive self-image

Result

Type 2, who is possessed by manipulation, who serves others in order to dominate and make himself indispensable, is being loosened up by the attitude of the fourth Enneagram type. This is because he has developed a feeling for himself and for his own needs and feelings. Type 2 takes on the characteristic features of Type 4 and enjoys his life, freeing himself from his unrealistic self-image—the martyr or the pleaser.

RELIEF POINT 4 → 1

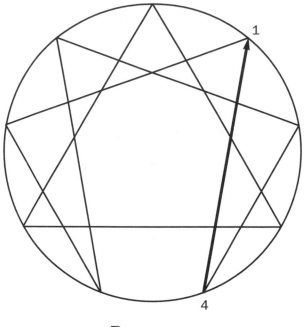

Processes

Line of sight in processes

As did the line of sight from the fourth to the second Enneagram point, the glance from the fourth to the first holds great danger.

The difficulties, which can increase at the fourth Enneagram point up to a point of desperation, make you want to look back and idealize the past. Indeed, you were better off at the first Enneagram point than here at the fourth. You could, at the first Enneagram point, ignore your situation, since you have lived for the most part in the area of illusion. You fooled yourself, and thus you felt subjectively better. These illusions now have slowly dissolved, and that is painful. But nevertheless, you need to continue to walk on the path you are on, since it promises the chance to reach a resolution to the problems that are now so hard on you.

THE RELAXED AFFLICTED PERSON

Key Words

Reference to reality through firm structures

End of emotional confusion through security

Characterization of this combination

Psychology

What comes from Type 4	What comes from Type 1
Loss of the reference to reality	Firm norms and systems
Confusion	Structure
Too great an identification with one's own feelings	Values instead of feelings

Result

Type 4, who thinks that he has gotten the short stick—even though he is something very special—finds his relief when he acquires the ways of behavior of Enneagram Point 1. The world of values, firm systems, and imagination from Type 1 gives Type 4, who often suffers from confusion, a structure and security that Type 4 longs for so much. Through the firm value systems of Type 1, Type 4 gets structure and wins a reference to reality, which, however, he loses easily again and again.

RELIEF POINT 5 → 8

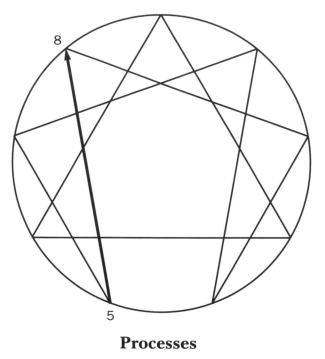

Processes

Line of sight in processes

At the fifth Enneagram point, you still experience your situation as being difficult. You have your goal clearly before your eyes, but at the same time it seems so far away as to be unreachable. If you look from the fifth Enneagram point to the eighth, then it becomes clear that you must hold firmly to your goal in order to proceed. At the same time, the goal in its completion appears so perfect that it exercises an enormous magnetism, which makes the searching person go on. It motivates him strongly to keep going, because he can see the freedom that is to be reached at the eighth Enneagram point, and how he is still suffering.

At this point, the lesson of the suffering—consciously taken upon oneself—begins to become clear.

THE RELAXED OBSERVER

Key Words

The introvert opens himself to the outside world.

Something is being done with accumulated knowledge.

Characterization of this combination

Psychology

What comes from Type 5	What comes from Type 8
The tendency to retreat	The turn to the outside
The accumulation of knowledge, without using it	Trying out all one's abilities in the outside world
	Unshakable self-confidence

Result

The retreating, shy Type 5, who only observes the course of the world, gets his harmonic balance through taking on some of the ways of behavior of the eighth Enneagram type. Type 8 is the active person who goes out into life in order to represent his values. He is self-confident and strong. This attitude is good for Enneagram Type 5 as the passive observer, since otherwise he runs the danger of suffocating on his knowledge. Type 5 must go out into the world and do something there with his knowledge. He must not keep it greedily for himself. A Type 5, who can go to the outside and convert his knowledge, is a happy and loose Observer.

161

RELIEF POINT 7 → 5

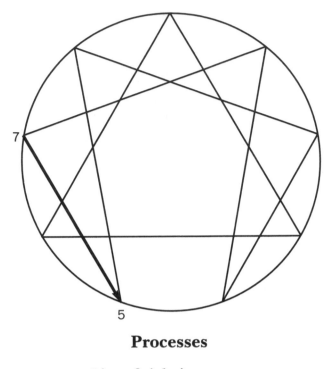

Processes

Line of sight in process

If you look from Point 7, the first step of the reached goal, to the fifth Enneagram point, then you can once again visualize how you have proceeded through the consciousness work. You see the progress you have made—by not suffering from your emotions anymore and no longer falling into immobilizing apathy—and by being able to consciously determine your life. That frequently motivates the searching person to go on to Enneagram Point 8.

THE RELAXED OPTIMIST

Key Words

Pausing and observing

First thinking and then acting

Observing precisely, instead of dissipating one's energies

Characterization of this combination

Psychology

What comes from Type 7	**What comes from Type 5**
Quick action, which is often triggered by fascination	Calm
	Ability to observe
Superficiality	Profundity
Tendency to dissipate one's energies	

Result

The flaky and superficial Type 7, who is always involved in all kinds of projects, finds his peace through the depth and peace of Type 5. Type 7 is too quickly fascinated and feels torn between many things. He finds his resting place by observing and reflecting, as is natural for Type 5. Most of the time, Type 7 acts before he has thought enough or received enough information. The turn toward Type 5 brings Type 7 harmony and balance and keeps him from dissipating his energies.

163

RELIEF POINT 8 → 2

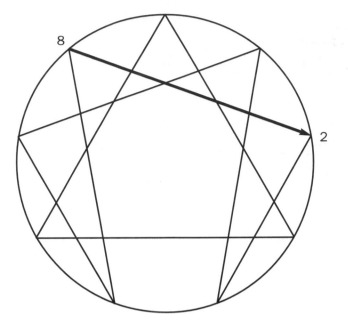

Processes

Line of sight in processes

If you look from the eighth Enneagram point to the second one, you will have the continuation of the process in mind, which is completed at this point on a new level. It becomes clear that, in the last analysis, you never reach your goal—in the sense that it doesn't go on anymore and you can just stay where you are. The Enneagram always goes on—it never stands still—and already it is causing you to take the possibility of a new development into consideration.

THE RELAXED BOSS

Key Words

Instead of will for power, perception of the needs of others

Instead of aggression and violence, response to the other person

Characterization of this combination

Psychology

What comes from Type 8	What comes from Type 2
Aggressiveness and violence	Empathy
The will to power	Willingness to serve
The overlooking of other people	Social abilities

Result

Type 8—who with his will to power, could have been created by Nietzsche—turns in happy situations into Type 2. Type 2, who can help others and wants to, softens the aggressive Type 8, who most of the time docs not even notice the other person. Through Type 2's characteristic features, Type 8 becomes more social and can scc thc possibility of partnership. The serving way of Type 2 also softens Type 8's open violence and aggressiveness. You can feel with the other one—a revolutionary idea for Type 8—which makes him happier than when he acts alone as the power person.

RELIEF POINT 3 → 6

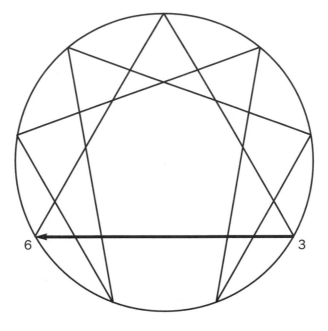

Processes

Line of sight in processes

The glance from the mechanical to the conscious shock point (from Enneagram Point 3 to Enneagram Point 6) makes it clear how essential is consciousness and will in the continuation of processes. Not any kind of impulse from the outside will do; there must be a conscious searching for the effective outside impulse. You have a certain question and search actively for the right book, the right teacher, whatever, that can help you to continue. The teaching at Enneagram Point 6 is that you must do something actively in order to proceed. The foundations for that were set at the third Enneagram point, and it is helpful to visualize these foundations once again.

166

THE RELAXED MAGICIAN

Key Words

Instead of career, loyalty to his task

Instead of fraud and deceit, integrity

Characterization of this combination

Psychology

What comes from Type 3	What comes from Type 6
Tendency to lying and deceit	Faithfulness
Career addiction	Loyalty
The showing of a mask	Integrity

Result

Type 3, who, when in doubt, uses fraud and deceit, finds in the overly correct sixth Enneagram type not only his counterimage, but also the type that is his natural opposite. Also, Type 3 lives in fear of being only his "persona" (the character mask) and having nothing left, except for success. The attitude of Type 6, doing faithfully his work without having to prove himself much, relaxes the constantly stressed Type 3.

RELIEF POINT 6 → 9

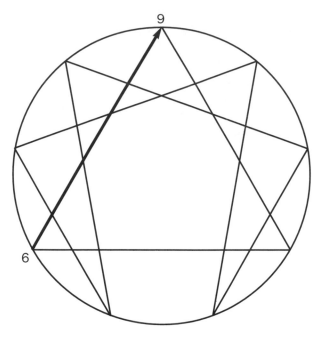

Processes

Line of sight in processes

If the searching person looks from the sixth to the ninth Enneagram point, he makes himself conscious of the fact that the journey through the Enneagram keeps going and does not come to a standstill. After this second outside impulse, a third one will follow at the ninth Enneagram point, which will let us enter into a new course in the process.

Furthermore, we can have in the line of sight a momentary vision of our ideal and completed task.

THE RELAXED HERO

Key Words

Instead of constant striving, the courage to be lazy

Instead of security, indolence

Characterization of this combination

Psychology

What comes from Type 6	What comes from Type 9
Constant striving for adaptation	Laziness and indolence
Search for security	Calm

Result

The always striving Hero of Type 6 finds its balance in the lazy calm of Type 9. Type 6 is always struggling to do things correctly, since he is anxious and must build up his security. Many things, on the other hand, do not matter to Type 9. He wants to have his peace and quiet, but it is much too exhausting for him to be afraid of anything. Type 6 can learn from Type 9 that things can also work out even if there doesn't seem to be any security—indeed, that you can live much looser, more merrily and well without it. Our society, though, supports the attitude of Type 6, and makes Type 9 out as being a lazy good-for-nothing. The correct mixture of Type 6 and 9 brings harmony into the life.

RELIEF POINT 9 → 3

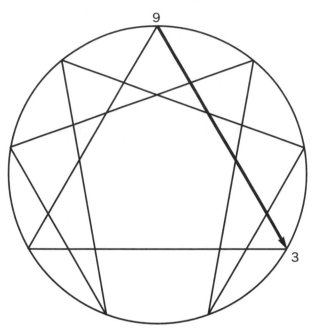

Processes

Line of sight in processes

If you look from the ninth Enneagram point to the third, you are already standing at the beginning of a new process, expecting to find the outside impulse that will accelerate it.

Since the glance is from the ninth to the third Enneagram point, it is not a glance back, but on the contrary, a vision of a new process.

THE RELAXED LOVER

Key Words

Effectiveness instead of laziness

Organization instead of dawdling away one's life

Characterization of this combination

Psychology

What comes from Type 9	What comes from Type 3
Laziness and idleness	Effectiveness
Aimlessness because of lack of interest	Know-how about career
	Delight in work

Result

The lazy Type 9 needs the more active Type 3 in order to keep him from sinking completely into the morass of passivity. From Type 3, Type 9 can learn how to create one's life aimfully, effectively, and actively, and can also see how much fun it can be. Everyone in our society needs at least a little success, and Type 3 shows Type 9 the way to get it.

171

7. The Combinations of the Individual Points

Each system of types has the problem, when you look closely, that only a few people correspond to one type exactly. The human character is very complex, and teachings of personality types take this into consideration by introducing mixed types.

All types of the Enneagram can mix with each other, except for the three basic types at the shock points—3, 6, and 9. Frequently, we behave differently from our main type, and also not like our stress or relief type. That has to do with our early childhood experiences (especially from our parents and grandparents), which became a model for our behavior in certain situations. That is the so-called "introjected" behavior—behavior that we learned from models in our youth—and that overlies our own Enneagram type.

Furthermore, our behavior can be overlaid by the Persona.

Definition: Persona

The Persona is a complicated system of relations between the individual consciousness and society. You can think of it as a kind of mask, which is calculated to make a certain impression on others at the same time as it covers up the person's real nature.[26]

You could also define the persona as the side of a person that is consciously represented as a mask.

The persona that we put on as a professional mask does not necessarily have to have something to do with our Enneagram type.

Through this persona overlay of the actual Enneagram type, and through the behavioral models of childhood, mixed types appear, which we'll take a closer look at in the following pages.

Following the Gurdjieff tradition, I will show, for the most part, only the problematic points of the mixed types, since we can learn from them and grow, as a result. So, don't get a shock. You already know your sunny side. Now you need to get to know your shadow side, so it won't cause any trouble for you.

American schools of the Enneagram use the concept of wings. This means that the type before and/or the type after the individual's type have a major influence. Followers of this system believe that only types that are next to each other can combine. I doubt this, because everyday life experience and Enneagram tests show that all types of the Enneagram can mix.

When we speak about combinations of types, we have to remember that every type can be lived and expressed on different levels of consciousness: free or blocked, healthy or neurotic, intellectual or feeling or sensual.

Unlike the followers of Oscar Ichazo, I come from the theory that a human being will often combine in himself the characteristic features of different types. I consider it rare to find a person who manifests only one type, as Ichazo, Richard Riso, Andreas Ebert, and Richard Rohr describe it. Gurdjieff sees the human being much more realistically as a creature with many different egos. Especially since Richard Riso came up with his rigid Enneagram theories, a myth developed that each person personifies only one type. Riso and also Rohr and Ebert say that they never mix. I consider that a highly theoretical and idealized statement that comes about because the followers of the personality types of the Enneagram understood only half the truth. They do not see that the Enneagram is a process model, which, among other things, contains a dynamic concept of types—not a theoretical and frozen doctrine that reveals the weak spots of others.

You will realize, if you want to allocate an Enneagram type to yourself, that most of the time you combine in yourself the characteristic features of two or sometimes more Enneagram types—or perhaps you cannot allocate any at all. Real people, luckily, do not correspond to the theories of a rigid doctrine of types. You will realize this when you look at different periods of your life. It is probable that you personified completely different Enneagram types at different times. According to Riso and Ichazo, that must not happen; otherwise, the whole idea of personality types becomes shaky.

The assumption that a person belongs to one Enneagram type all his life—or even at one point in time—is totally unjustified. Our motivations, needs, and talents are too complex to be absorbed completely in one single Enneagram type. The nine Enneagram types rather represent archetypal behavior patterns that can mix and overlay each other easily in a real person. Real people consist of at least two Enneagram types, as Goethe's Faust realized with his famous moan, "Two souls live, oh dear, in my breast." Real people act and observe the world from different points of view, and these depend on which ego has supremacy at the moment, and which ones share the leadership. Only in fully developed individuals do the inner forces of the human being follow only one motivation and one ego. Since, most likely, almost all readers of this book, like myself, have not reached this high state of development, I believe that a mixture of at least two types is much closer to real people than the assumption of only one type.

Students of Helen Palmer like to divide each type into one of three subtypes: social, sexual, and survival. The person with the social orientation either likes to be active in groups or hates them. He is often concerned with abstract political or social ideas. The sexual subtype is communicative and concerned with relationships. The survival subtype is concerned with his own wellbeing and is often cautious. Of course, this is only one of the ways you can differentiate the Enneagram types. How we differentiate them—forming subtypes—depends on what we want to analyze. It is important to keep in mind that when we speak of the combination of types, each one can be expressed on different levels.

In the following pages, I consider a mixture of the different Enneagram types that I believe comes closer to reality than the rigid interpretation of types.

Type 1 and Type 2

What is reinforced

Both types would like to reach perfection. The first Enneagram type tries to approach perfection through correctness. The second Enneagram type tries to approach it through social behavior. Both can therefore be very much convinced of their view of the world. In addition, they both restrain themselves from showing aggression. They usually express it indirectly.

What contradicts itself

If the first Enneagram type is concerned with general values—such as perfection—especially in the material world, the second Enneagram type is concerned with personal values and with recognition from others. Enneagram Type 1 is concerned mainly with himself and his opinions, while Type 2 can put himself into other people's situations, which he does constantly.

Result

The combination of the first two Enneagram types leads to a type who thinks that he represents objective values. He claims that he is thinking of the needs of others, of the greatest good for the greatest many. He pretends to know your needs before you know what they are, and often poses as a great and perfect helper. This may make him seem cold and impersonal.

When he doesn't like something, at first he becomes moralistic and reproachful, since he is not able to convince others through his good nature—and if that still doesn't help, he expresses his aggression indirectly.

This type is able to deal with daily life easily. Ebert and Rohr call it hypocritical and controlling, but also, in the case of evolved people, compassionate.

Frequency

This type is found fairly frequently, especially in large companies and large cities.

174

Type 1 and Type 3

What is reinforced

Enneagram Types 1 and 3 meet in their efficiency. Both know how to work hard. Type 1, however, is more concerned with material matters or basic ethical values, while Type 3 seeks general recognition. But the strategies it takes to reach their goals are the same for the two Enneagram types—efficiency.

What contradicts itself

Though they share ways of behaving, these two Enneagram types are concerned with completely different values. Type 1 is righteous and honest in his enterprises. But Type 3 is not very interested in these values. Actually, they get in his way when he wants to reach his goal—success—quickly. Therefore, we can often find him involved in shady business deals, where there is fraud and deceit. Type 1 would never let himself be carried away into something like that. It would deeply offend his moral sensibilities.

Result

This combination type is hard-working, and, most of the time, succeeds in reaching his goal. On the way to this goal, he often is tempted by illegal dealings that fascinate him, but which he rejects, strictly due to fear.

Frequency

This type is not common.

175

Type 1 and Type 4

What is reinforced

The bewitched (unevolved) emotions of Enneagram Type 1, which leads to constant activity, an obsession with criticism, and dogmatic arguments, are actually enhanced by the unstable emotionality of Enneagram Type 4. When they combine, the result is a vulnerable, very unstable type who often allows himself to be carried away into over-hasty decisions and actions. The first, just like the fourth Enneagram Type, can be intensely dogmatic. Both types are inclined to be aggressive.

What contradicts itself

Type 1 thinks of himself as the spokesman for a group, while Type 4 thinks of himself as an isolated individualist.

The Enneagram Type 1 frequently reveals a good deal of discipline, while the fourth Enneagram type is rather undisciplined, which has to do with his moods.

Result

Either this mixed type is determined by the ups and downs of Type 4—in which case he is often depressed and frequently frighteningly self-destructive—or he reacts in stress situations thoughtlessly, mindlessly, and over-hastily. He seems to the outside world like a moody critic who is always finding "a hair in the soup."

If, in this mixed type, the discipline of

Type 1 dominates, we find a perfectionist who is often haunted by the fear of poverty. He gets his strength through the creative power of Type 4. Even though his perfectionism sometimes makes the creations of this mixed type somewhat unpopular, most of the time he fascinates those around him with his creativity, which he often expresses in interior design or architecture.

Frequency

This mixed type is very common.

Type 1 and Type 5

What is reinforced

Enneagram Type 1 and Type 5 are basically inhibited. This is obvious in Type 5, with his shy, reserved manner, while the inhibition in Type 1 is not so noticeable. But you can see it in his addiction to criticism and his dogmatic ways, with which he keeps people at arm's length.

These two Enneagram types also show a tendency toward perfectionism. Type 1 is concerned with perfection in the material world, which represents his own values, and Type 5 is interested in perfection in the accumulation of knowledge. For him, knowledge always has to be as complete as possible.

What contradicts itself

While Type 1 can act and assert himself without any difficulty, Type 5 is astonishingly passive and weak in asserting himself, when it counts.

While Type 1 is inclined to criticize the opinions of others, Type 5 behaves completely differently. He finds other opinions interesting, and as a rememberer and collector of knowledge, he listens to them with interest in order to absorb them into his knowledge storehouse. Because of that, Type 5 does not necessarily have fixed opinions of his own, and even if he had, he would not present them in a provocative way.

Result

We can call this mixed type the Inhibited Perfectionist, who often wanders as an unworldly specialist through his life. He also seems to be socially inhibited, sort of "wooden."

In any case, most of the time, this mixed type is very intelligent.

Frequency

This type occurs often in academic circles. You'll find many of them in universities, for example, even though the type is relatively rare.

177

Type 1 and Type 6

What is reinforced

Enneagram Types 1 and 6 are both looking for security. Type 1 tries to achieve this security through perfection in the material world, while Type 6 tries to achieve security through willpower and patience.

In his faithfulness to an idea or a thing, Type 6 is just as stubborn as Type 1 is in his material preoccupation. The sixth and first Enneagram types are both very independent and usually go their own way.

What contradicts itself

While the first Enneagram type is, for the most part, bound to the material world and easily dominated by his feelings, the sixth Enneagram point stands at the transition from the emotional to the intellectual area of the Enneagram. From this position, he succeeds in observing himself and his environment fairly objectively.

The first Enneagram type rarely succeeds in doing that.

Result

The result of the mixture of these two Enneagram types could be a perfect manager, who works for a powerful institution and represents it in the outside world. The press secretary of a government or a political party, for example, could belong to this type.

In the negative case, this mixed type does not find the security he seeks. He is haunted by fears of poverty, feels that he is out of place everywhere and that he is employed in a job that is beneath him.

Frequency

This type is relatively rare. In evolved form, as I pointed out before, he may be the speaker for a large institution. In his unevolved state, he is found with great frequency—unfortunately.

Type 1 and Type 7

What is reinforced

Enneagram Type 1 and Type 7 both have an inclination to impulsive action, and they are both highly susceptible to stress.

Type 7 thinks of the world as being a pleasant, large playpen, a meadow in which all people can play, according to their desire and mood.

Type 1 also has utopian ideas, which usually have a material element in them, but he does not share the carefree nature of Type 7.

What contradicts itself

Basically, we can see two completely different types in the first and seventh Enneagram types. The perfectionistic Type 1 contrasts perfectly with the playful Type 7, for whom perfection means nothing but strain. In this mixed type, indolence and perfection meet each other. Striving for perfection is completely foreign to Type 7, since he is used to creating a lot of things that are not necessarily perfect. He is a maker, putting emphasis on pleasure/lust. This attitude only disgusts Type 1.

Result

If, in this mixed type, Type 7 is stronger, then the addiction to perfection of the first Enneagram type is lessened. At the same time, the bold superficiality of Type 7 is weakened by the way Type 1 strives for perfection, and, in the most favorable cases, a balance between the two extremes come about.

But most of the time, in this mix, a blind flight away from suffering comes about. This mixed type searches, like one obsessed, for a lucky break, which he often finds in the media. Especially in the editorial staff of newspapers, in broadcasting and television, with its hectic activities, this mixed type feels very comfortable and can also work well and with recognition.

Frequency

It is rare to find a mixed type who has found a middle path. When you do, it is probably the result of successful therapy or a product of old age, in which life's experiences mitigate the extremes. You will find the type who acts successfully in the public eye more frequently.

179

Type 1 and Type 8

What is reinforced

The first and the eighth Enneagram types can both become fanatical about their goals. While Type 1 takes on the critical, dogmatic part, Type 8 takes on the aggressive expression, which he fights through with strength and without considering his losses. Both, in their power game, do not see the other one at all—and also lose themselves. It is clear to everyone, except to the ones participating, that such a power game can cover up anxieties and compensate for a great deal.

What contradicts itself

The first Enneagram type, in his game, which he takes much too seriously, is concerned primarily with material security. Type 8, though, concentrates only on the enforcement and the feeling of his own strength and power. He is, in contrast to Type 1, only poorly able to criticize, since he doesn't notice others at all.

Result

In this explosive mixture, fanatical extremes sometimes result. Here, the passion to criticize easily combines with aggression, which can go as far as violence. This type can fanatically put down the opinions of other people. The loss of security is often the trigger for this unpleasant mixture.

Frequency

This mixed type is found more and more frequently throughout the world, suggesting radical action in the "solution" of social conflicts. Germany knows this type more than well enough, but it can also be found increasingly in Islam, the Balkans, and in Israel.

Type 1 and Type 9

What is reinforced

At the first and ninth Enneagram type, little is reinforced because they are so different. You might say at the most, that the perfection for which Type 1 strives is lived by Enneagram Type 9 in self-contented peace. But Type 9 perfection is completely different from the one that Type 1 seeks.

What contradicts itself

Enneagram Type 1 and Enneagram Type 9 differ in astonishingly clear ways. The peace-loving Type 9, bent on harmony, is a perfect counterpart to the criticizing, dogmatic Type 1, who is bent on material goods. The first Enneagram type is turned towards the outside and is a physical type, while the ninth Enneagram type is a perception/feeling type, turned toward the inside. Thus, Type 1 is active and fast; Type 9 is passive and slow.

The perfect economizing of Type 1 would mean too much expenditure for Type 9 and would disrupt his quiet coziness.

In all these central points, the two Enneagram types differ fundamentally.

Result

In the best case, from the mixture of these two different brothers, a new type comes about—one who is able to stand up for such important values as harmony, calm (instead of haste), and peaceableness. Rohr and Ebert named this the "redeemed nine-wing of the first Enneagram type"—a fair person.

In the worst cases, which in my experience is the most common form of this mixed type, we have an intolerant and, at the same time, lazy person in front of us, who grumbles his way through life and does not get anything done—from which he suffers.

Also the prejudiced person, who is selfish, belongs to this mixed type.

Frequency

According to my experience, this mixed type does not occur frequently. When he is an evolved person, he represents the so-called humanist who may occur today as a wise teacher, thoughtful journalist, or culture critic.

We find the unevolved mixed type, from time to time, in young people whom psychologists call borderline narcissists, who hang around passively, finding fault with everything.

181

Type 2 and Type 3

What is reinforced

The second as well as the third Enneagram point can work hard in order to achieve his goals, but those goals are very different. Type 2 wants to get power by being indispensable, while Type 3 strives for a career that is visible to the outside.

The fact that they are both calculating connects the two Enneagram types. Type 2 often acts in order to get recognition, and most of the time he does it so skillfully that people do not realize what he is doing. He brings beauty into the world and wants to make himself popular through it—and he frequently succeeds.

Type 3 is a master calculator: How fast can he get a career, how can he build up his image, and how can he attain success?

Both the second and the third Enneagram point are characterized by their adaptability.

What contradicts itself

The second Enneagram type is, for the most part, oriented toward others and open to them, while the third Enneagram type is obsessed with his ego.

As mentioned before, these two Enneagram types are very calculating, though in a most contrary way. Type 3 strives for success completely openly, or, if he does not get to the desired success that way, he pushes on with fraud and dishonesty. Type 2, on the other hand, is a flatterer, who remains in the background and does not need the limelight, the way Type 3 does.

Result

This mixed type can be called calculating and deceitful. He is a master in the planning and use of strategies, and therefore he does not walk a straight path. He is driven by his will to power.

But in his evolved form, this type can also be sociable and amiable. He is pleasant, "nice," and friendly, and only in emergencies does he take extreme advantage of the other person/people in his relationships.

Rohr and Ebert speak here of the "adapted" type, who forms the three-wing of Type 2.

Frequency

You can find this mixed type in an unevolved form very frequently among politicians on all levels. You probably need a certain amount of this mix to move up in political parties.

The more evolved form occurs more frequently in older people.

Type 2 and Type 4

What is reinforced

The second and fourth Enneagram types both show a tendency to self-aggression, but they express it very differently. It is also common to both Enneagram types that they are not able to associate comfortably with others. For Type 2, the pretended approaching of others is a compensation for his feelings of inferiority; actually, he is missing the necessary emotional depth. Type 4 has dealings only with the unreachable; that which is attainable does not interest him.

These two Enneagram types lose themselves easily, which is the reason why the exercise of self-remembering is particularly necessary for them.

What contradicts itself

Type 2 can keep his eyes on his goal for a long time, and can steer for it consistently. That is impossible for Type 4, since he, dependent on his moods, often floats back and forth like a leaf in the wind. He is a plaything for his emotions. He cannot adapt himself, since he is convinced that he is special and extraordinary. In contrast, Type 2 easily gives in to the practical and beautiful, and adapts himself to the practical reality.

Result

On one hand, this mixed type can be completely obsessed by receiving recognition and love through service. If he does not reach his goal, he directs his energy against himself, even up to suicide attempts. Since he can only with difficulty associate with others, he often goes through life unhappily, and he does that with a substantial amount of self-pity, which can frighten off others.

But this mixed type also appears in an evolved form, through which he becomes conscious of himself. He can sketch himself as a "beautiful soul" and also live this ideal. Such an evolved mixed type is also capable of living his life happily.

Frequency

This mixed type can be found fairly frequently in its "bewitched" (unevolved) form, but very rarely in its evolved form.

Type 2 and Type 5

What is reinforced

The second, as well as the fifth Enneagram type, seems to be fairly reserved. At Type 2, the cause for this is his lack of emotional depth, which makes him seem rather aloof. Type 5 is a distanced person, who works from the background.

Both Enneagram types have the capacity for precise observation. Type 5 lives this capability to excess, while Type 2 uses it for a purpose. Type 2 observes in order to be able to serve the other person. Type 5, on the other hand, observes in order to satisfy his thirst for knowledge, which gives him the security he needs.

What contradicts itself

Type 2 is rather naive and active. Type 5, on the other hand, is passive and brooding. The second Enneagram type is not usually as smart as Type 5. The unevolved Type 2 is often superficial and vain, and does not think very deeply. Type 5 is smart, often very educated, and frequently intellectual; Type 2 is like that only in exceptional cases.

Result

From this mixture, we get a good observer, who realizes precisely what is happening and who knows how to use his chances. But he avoids standing out, since it is easier to manipulate from the background.

Frequency

This mixed type does not occur frequently.

Type 2 and Type 6

What is reinforced

Type 2 and 6 meet in their serving of others. While Type 2, through his service, gradually takes over the power, Type 6 serves unselfishly and loyally. He is the faithful server, who would not in his wildest dreams try to take power away from his master.

Both Enneagram types seek security, which Type 2 wants to get through making others dependent upon him. The sixth Enneagram type hopes to receive this security as a reward for his loyalty and faithfulness.

What contradicts itself

The second Enneagram type turns against his "master," while the sixth Enneagram type helps him and stands by his side. The sixth Enneagram type truly serves, while Type 2 only seems to.

Result

These two Enneagram types result in a person who is completely geared toward security, who makes himself dependent easily on all kinds of institutions, and is caught in a net of unrespectable business associates. Even though this type, in his unevolved form, may serve in an institution, he is torn by doubts as to whether that will bring him enough security. As a result, he serves faithfully and loyally, on one hand, while on the other he plays with the idea of taking over the power secretly, quietly, and calmly. These are only fantasies, but they torture the upright Type 6 soul to whom that which is not allowed cannot be tolerated.

Frequency

You can find this type frequently in our society. The insurance and security business thrives on irrational anxieties and striving for safety.

185

Type 2 and Type 7

What is reinforced

The second and seventh Enneagram types have little in common. Both work rather hysterically in extreme situations, since they tend to overreact.

What contradicts itself

The second Enneagram type is introverted, while Type 7 operates, blithely unconcerned, in the outside world—in fact, he downright needs the outside world.

Type 7 is an action type, with the emphasis on pleasure/lust, who does not take anything too seriously. The second Enneagram type, on the other hand, can remain without problems his whole life, as long as he has one thing that gives him security. For Type 7, that means dependency, and he equates that dependency with insecurity.

Result

The mixture of the second and the seventh Enneagram types represents a person who acts quickly, and who manipulates others with his actions; most of the time he does this unconsciously. But since he displays a certain childishness, people often let his machinations slide, because, after all, he did not really mean it in a bad way. How calculating he really is becomes clear only much later, and by then this mixed type has long gotten away with it.

Frequency

This mixed type is relatively rare.

Type 2 and Type 8

What is reinforced

Type 2 and Type 8 know exactly what they want. And both are also totally determined to reach their goals, no matter what.

What contradicts itself

In order to reach his goal, Type 8 uses aggression and violence, while Type 2 chooses the indirect path of flattery and manipulation. He never proceeds, as Type 8 does, with his elbows in open aggression; he is too insecure to do it. He is, after all, lacking in the strength and self-confidence of Type 8.

Result

In its unevolved form, this mixed type can destroy in a blind rage what he has worked for over a long period of time. This tendency to destroy what is important to him makes him suffer terribly.

In the evolved form, the strength of Type 8 and the social cleverness of Type 2 come together, so that he can show consideration for the needs of others without having to repress his own needs while doing it.

Frequency

This combination does not exist very frequently.

187

Type 2 and Type 9

What is reinforced

The second, as well as the ninth Enneagram Type, can easily step into another person's shoes, which is why both types are often asked for advice.

Both types are concerned with harmony, but the harmony used by Type 2 is a means of gaining power, which is foreign to the ninth Enneagram point.

What contradicts itself

Type 2 wants to dominate through his behavior, while that is much too exhausting for Type 9, who would rather just have peace and quiet and is little interested in power.

Also, Type 9 does not want to serve, like Type 2, but rather wants to live his own life in peace and harmony.

Result

In its evolved form, this mixed type is a classic helper, who brings other people to harmony. He can have a very soothing effect on others who are in stressful situations.

In its unevolved form, this mixed type is a lazy person, who crawls through life by exploiting others. Often he is a master of making other people feel guilty, and then he uses their bad conscience for his own purposes.

Frequency

The unevolved form exists more frequently than the evolved form, in my experience.

Type 3 and Type 4

What is reinforced

Type 3 and 4 have relatively little in common. In the Enneagram according to Gurdjieff, they must both learn to deal with their feelings more consciously. The third Enneagram type represses his feelings by concentrating on his career, while the fourth Enneagram type is completely powerless against his feelings.

Both Enneagram types also want to be something special: Type 4 has no doubt that he is special and extraordinary, and Type 3 strives to be extraordinary through his success and the image he presents.

Type 3 and Type 4 both tend to self-aggression, which expresses itself in Type 3 in workaholism, and in Type 4 in addictive behavior.

What contradicts itself

While Type 3 is a disciplined worker, extremely oriented toward success, discipline represents a very special challenge for Type 4. When Type 3 reaches his goal, he overidentifies with his success and becomes the personification of it; then, like Faust, he has sold his soul.

Result

It is very important for this mixed type to be regarded as something special and extraordinary, and for that he will put up with any kind of hardship. On the other hand, he becomes completely unstable and moody when he does not reach his goal.

According to Rohr and Ebert, this mixed type is, in its unevolved form, an arrogant braggart, and in his evolved form, an intuitive. Most of the time, this mixed type is demanding and not satisfied with the usual and the "normal."

Frequency

This mixed type occurs in our society as show-offs and braggarts, especially among the yuppies of large cities.

189

Type 3 and Type 5

What is reinforced

These two Enneagram types are so foreign to each other that, in my opinion, there are no essential aspects that are reinforced in them.

What contradicts itself

Looked at more closely, these two Enneagram types contradict themselves on all levels:

1. Type 3 is addicted to his career.
   Type 5 is a retreated observer.

2. Type 3 is highly active.
   Type 5 is passive.

3. Type 3 is extraverted.
   Type 5 is introverted.

4. Type 3 is image conscious.
   Type 5 is shy.

5. Type 3 is inclined to deceit.
   Type 5 is honest.

This list could be continued—these are only the most noticeable differences between these two Enneagram types.

Result

In very rare cases, we find this mixed type in universities as researchers, who occasionally also enforce their career, and then retreat again immediately.

Frequency

Since these two Enneagram types are so different, a mixture almost never occurs, since it would create an almost schizoid character.

Type 3 and Type 7

What is reinforced

Type 3 and Type 7 can be very similar. They both show:

1. a lot of activity

2. a high orientation toward performance

3. pronounced extroverted behavior

What contradicts itself

While Type 3 does his thing with seriousness, Type 7 plays. Type 7 really follows the advice of Gurdjieff—to take life as a game—even though he does not necessarily do that consciously.

While Type 3 is, most of the time, concerned with his career, Type 7 is an astonishing optimist. He simply assumes that he will be successful and only half-heartedly strives for it.

Type 7 emphasizes pleasure/lust, while Type 3 puts the emphasis on work.

Result

In the evolved form, the mixed type is a playful, ingenious person, who has luck in life and finds recognition in his profession. In groups, he can electrify other members through his optimism, and most of the time he is versed in many fields.

In the unevolved form, he is a superficial dilettante, who will do anything to move up, and whose means are not always very fair.

Frequency

This type occurs rarely.

191

Type 3 and Type 8

What is reinforced

The third as well as the eighth Enneagram type both want to see success and are willing to do everything to get it. Both can work hard and they know their goals exactly. They are capable of concentrating all their forces on the reaching of this goal.

The third and the eighth Enneagram point both show off an astonishing self-confidence, which can be shaken up only with difficulty. Both are very ego-oriented and don't care about the needs of others.

What contradicts itself

Whereas the third Enneagram type uses, if need be, fraud and deceit in order to reach his goal, the eighth Enneagram point devotes himself more to violence and open aggression. He is frequently concerned with pushing through his values, which he considers essential for humankind. Type 3, on the other hand, is not concerned with humankind, but solely with his personal career and his image.

Result

This mixed type is extremely success-oriented and knows exactly how he can achieve this success. Nothing can stop him, and he identifies so much with his successes that he completely forgets himself. If, however, success does not happen, then this mixed type runs the risk of using criminal means to reach the goal.

He can work extremely hard and is classified by the outside world as workaholic. His strength and his neglect of the rights and the needs of others, makes this type seem unappealing, which often leads to his isolation. He often lives alone, since he cannot tolerate any restrictions.

Frequency

This mixed type occurs relatively frequently, especially in today's business community. To a degree, he is also admired in our society.

Type 4 and Type 5

What is reinforced

The fourth and the fifth Enneagram type both show the tendency to retreat, especially in difficult situations. Both Enneagram types live mainly their introverted side.

The fourth and fifth Enneagram type fight constantly against their feelings. At Type 4 that shows in his notorious moods, and at Type 5 in his retreat, which makes him unapproachable.

The strength of these types lies in their sensitive observation of their environment and those in it.

What contradicts itself

While the fourth Enneagram type can deal creatively and actively with his knowledge, Type 5 is not inclined to use his knowledge at all, and keeps it for himself.

While Type 4 thinks that he is something special and extraordinary, Type 5 thinks that he is relatively normal and shows no special inclination to grandiosity. He prefers to remain unobtrusively in the background and seems more adapted than extraordinary.

Result

Mixed types often seem extremely unapproachable and mysterious. They are introverted to such an extent that they often have few friends and live fairly lonely lives. But they do not suffer from loneliness, unless Type 4 is the stronger part. In that case, they envy people who are able to make contacts easily and who have many friends.

Dealing with this mixed type is not easy, since he often is quite vulnerable and sensitive to his environment. He can be extremely creative, and when the Type 4 aspect is strongly developed, he can use this creativity successfully in his profession.

Rohr and Ebert distinguish three different 4 Types with a five-wing:

1. The unevolved mixed type who shuts himself off from the outside world.

2. The normal mixed type who has a mysterious effect on his environment.

3. The evolved type who is creative.

They characterize 5 Types with a four-wing as giving the impression of being:

1. inspired when evolved

2. sensitive when normal

3. hopeless when unevolved

Frequency

We find this mixed type frequently in creative professions, and especially in the environment of artists.

Type 4 and Type 6

What is reinforced

Type 4 and Type 6 meet, despite all their differences, in their search for security. Both dream of a secure life; their attempts to reach it, though, are very different.

What contradicts itself

While Type 4 can only with great difficulty submit to serving others, Type 6 does not find it hard at all. He is happy when he can serve another person faithfully. Type 4 will only try serving when in greatest need, and he immediately finds that it conflicts with his image of himself. Usually this ends in great hostility toward the person that he is serving.

It is also difficult for Type 4 to be faithful. Closeness and familiarity cause him anxiety, and therefore he is often most faithful in a long-distance relationship.

Result

This mixed type is in a constant search for security, which he never reaches in the long run. His unstable feelings do not permit a longer lasting security to come about.

He often vacillates between closeness and distance, which does not make him and his partner especially happy. He is usually characterized by others as a "difficult person."

Frequency

This mixed type does not occur very frequently.

Type 4 and Type 7

What is reinforced

Type 4 and Type 7 are very different. Nevertheless, they meet in their creativity. In fact, we could consider this mixture the creative pole of the Enneagram, where the feeling for aesthetics of Type 4 combines with the magical inspiration of Type 7.

Both Enneagram types have their ideals, but they live them very differently.

What contradicts itself

The lightness of the seventh Enneagram type is completely foreign to Type 4, who goes through life in a melancholy way. Suffering, from which Type 7 flees like the plague, is a constant companion of Type 4, who accepts it and does not try to repress it.

The superficial optimism of Type 7 is a mystery to Type 4, just as the suffering of Type 4 is incomprehensible to Type 7.

Result

This mixed type has an enormous potential for creativity. The lightness of Type 7 mitigates the heaviness of Type 4, and the profundity of Type 4 makes the superficiality of Type 7 tolerable. But at the same time it is hard for this mixed type to stabilize himself emotionally; he is strangely faltering and ungrounded.

When evolved, he lives between the poles of heavenly jubilation and grieving to death. In his euphoric phase, he gets his creative pushes, which he tries to bring into reality through hectic activity.

Frequency

This type is relatively rare, and like most of the mixed types that have some Type 4 in them, it can be found in artistic circles.

Type 4 and Type 8

What is reinforced

Most of the time Type 4 and Type 8 cannot stand each other at all, but they have a lot in common. Both are convinced of their special position in society. Type 8 is not generally conscious of this at all, and he rejects the show Type 4 puts on about being extraordinary. But this belief corresponds to his shadow (if anyone is allowed to be extraordinary, then he should be the one!). Type 8 acts as if he was the master over all others, and when another person also dares to be something special, he must reject that claim.

What contradicts itself

There is almost no greater contradiction than that between the highly sensitive Type 4 and the completely insensitive Type 8. Where Type 4 feels weak, Type 8 feels strong. And the aggression that the eighth Enneagram type shows towards the outside world corresponds to the self-aggression of Type 4, who always turns aggression inside. Type 8 is for Type 4 simply too brutal, unaesthetic, and much too loud. Type 8 thinks of Type 4 as an oversensitive screwball, unworldly, and snivelling.

Result

The combination of these different forces produces an unstable, aggressive mixed type who reacts aggressively in one situation and at another time with sensitivity. He is a mystery for his environment, and very unpredictable.

Frequency

This type is relatively rare.

Type 4 and Type 9

What is reinforced

Type 4 and Type 9 show a tendency to sensuality and often seem to be a bit unstable.

They are peace-loving, and strive for the highest degree of harmony, which is not granted to them frequently.

What contradicts itself

The moody side of Type 4 stands opposite the harmonious side of Type 9, whose peace would be disturbed by too much moodiness. Also the self-aggression of Type 4 is a mystery to Type 9, who wants to have a good life and to live with himself and others in peace.

Result

If the ninth Enneagram type is more strongly pronounced in this combination, then this mixed type can at least from time to time enjoy his life in an extremely lazy and idle way. In addition, he can make peace with himself, but this balance does not often last long, since his emotions vacillate a great deal and unfortunately destroy his harmony again and again. He often reacts to that with a certain bitterness or whining, which can put off others.

Frequency

This combination does not occur very frequently.

Type 5 and Type 6

What is reinforced

Neither the fifth nor the sixth Enneagram type are very oriented toward the outside, since they show a tendency to mistrust.

Both are very industrious.

What contradicts itself

The sixth Enneagram type does not have restraints on his actions, as Type 5 does. Because Type 5 is so dependent on his feelings, he has problems with loyalty and faithfulness. Since his feelings vacillate, his attitudes toward others can change accordingly.

Result

Most of the time this mixed type retreats and works industriously. Not rarely, he reveals a bitterness that makes him seem unhappy. He feels that he has gotten the short end of the stick and regards his fellow human beings distrustfully. In the unevolved form, this mixed type seems arrogant and presumptuous, but this is just a cover-up for his insecurity.

In his evolved form, the mixed type can approach problems with expertise and sympathetic understanding, and most of the time, he finds an astonishingly impressive and appealing solution.

Frequency

This mixed type is not so rare.

Type 5 and Type 7

What is reinforced

Even though Type 5 and Type 7 contrast with each other in a big way, they nevertheless get along very well most of the time. The extent of the knowledge of Type 5 corresponds to the different fields of knowledge of Type 7. Even though the knowledge at Type 5 is in depth, and at Type 7 in width, both nevertheless have extensive knowledge in common.

What contradicts itself

The great difference between these two Enneagram types lies in their ability to take action. Type 5 is positively inhibited about it, while Type 7 is action-oriented. Where the seventh Enneagram type acts hectically, Type 5 retreats into passivity.

Also, the reserve of Type 5 is completely foreign to Type 7, who places himself radiantly out in the world, which he enchants with his optimism.

Result

The evolved form of this mixed type can act very competently, since the often blind activism of Type 7 is mitigated by the precise observation of Type 5. In addition, the Type 5 portion is able to get solid information about the kind of action that is available to him, which the Type 7 portion can apply easily from his overview of many fields of knowledge.

In the unevolved form, this type can easily dissipate his energies in actions that degenerate into aimless activities. He can be extremely nervous and cannot follow any goal for a long time.

Frequency

Both forms of this mixed type are infrequent.

Type 5 and Type 8

What is reinforced

Type 5 and type 8 are very contrary, and there are no common characteristic features that could reinforce each other.

What contradicts itself

Both Enneagram types contradict themselves in more or less all important points.

1. Type 5 is reserved and quiet. Type 8 is overbearing and loud.

2. Type 5 is an objective observer. Type 8 often does not even really notice his environment.

3. Type 5 does not like to take action. Type 8 is extremely action-friendly.

4. Type 5 has a great amount of knowledge. Type 8 has strength and self-confidence.

Result

In the unevolved case, this rare mixed type shows a high readiness for aggression, and seems, at the same time, brooding and highly dissatisfied—or torn on the inside. He often retreats completely, and then turns back to the world again aggressively.

In the evolved form, we have here a mixed type who can market his enormous knowledge very well.

Frequency

This mixed type seems to exist very rarely.

Type 5 and Type 9

What is reinforced

Both Enneagram types seem passive and would rather just look at the world than interfere with its happenings.

Both types love harmony and are rarely aggressive.

What contradicts itself

Type 5 does not show the laziness of Type 9.

Result

The mixed type steps into the world in a relatively balanced way. He rests in himself, and is satisfied with himself and with the world.

In the unevolved state, though, he is very lazy and prefers to do nothing at all.

Frequency

This mixed type is relatively rare.

Type 6 and Type 7

What is reinforced

The sixth and seventh Enneagram type can be very warm and capable of approaching other people. That is the strength of these types, which is even increased in this mixture.

Both Enneagram types can be engaged in working for higher values and can seem merry and joyful towards the outside world.

What contradicts itself

Type 7 has problems remaining with a thing, person, or task, while that is exactly the strength of Type 6—his faithfulness.

Result

This mixed type is an unconcerned, friendly, warm-hearted and mostly humorous human being who walks easily through life, loved by everyone. He associates with others and takes on tasks successfully, but in conflict situations he becomes a bit hysterical and panicky. The problem of this type is his addiction to recognition, a driving factor in his life.

In the unevolved form, this mixed type can be defensive and grumpy and thus frighten off other people.

Frequency

This mixed type occurs frequently.

Type 6 and Type 8

What is reinforced

Type 6 and Type 8 are very foreign to each other. At the most, you could say that both are concerned with security. Type 8 searches for it in his ability to assert himself, while Type 6 finds it in his ability to be loyal and faithful.

What contradicts itself

Type 6 sees the other person and can help him and give him advice.

Type 8, on the other hand, sees only himself. Values like faithfulness and loyalty, which characterize Type 6, are for him only words. The eighth Enneagram type is characterized by the pushing through of his ideas and interests.

While Type 8 is an insensitive elbowing person, Type 6 is able to enter into other people's views with sensitivity. Type 8 overlooks the needs of others.

Result

This mixed type can be a smart businessman who serves his company and who is very useful. Especially in the personnel department, this mixed type can develop to his full capacity, since there he can dominate, but also use his intuition for the needs of others.

Despite a usually brilliant career, this type sometimes gets frightened that he could lose his security, and that his strength could change into neediness and weakness.

Frequency

This mixed type exists rarely.

Type 7 and Type 8

What is reinforced

The readiness to take action connects Type 7 and Type 8. Both types need to take action to keep from getting depressed.

The types are connected by their self-confidence.

What contradicts itself

Of course, Type 8 is completely lacking in the lightness of Type 7.

He seems strained and concentrated, while Type 7 is loose and intuitive.

Type 7 does not need, as the eighth Enneagram type does, to make a path through life with fists and elbows; everything runs easily and smoothly for him. Statistics show that Type 7 is the modern type of manager, whereas Type 8 represents the old-fashioned kind of "Boss."

Result

The mixed type is often mobile and smart in business. He is quite capable of asserting himself with all the means at his command, and nevertheless is popular due to his uncomplicated manner. Rohr and Ebert speak of the strength of his leadership and magnanimity.

But if in an unevolved form, this mixed type is avaricious and choleric and no longer so uncomplicated and friendly. In fact, he seems rather hostile and aggressive.

Frequency

This mixed type is not found very frequently.

Type 7 and Type 9

What is reinforced

Type 7 and Type 9 are connected with each other through the principle of lust, in which they are both involved. Lust and harmony are their basic life concerns.

What contradicts itself

Type 7 is not lazy and idle at all like Type 9, but he needs his daily portion of "action" in order to remain the "sunny boy." For type 9, such a life would be much too exhausting.

Result

This mixed type can produce harmony around him and, most of the time, is very popular. In case of the unevolved type, a dis-interest in everything may take over and some kind of nihilism may be present.

Frequency

This type occurs more frequently
in the evolved form.

Type 8 and Type 9

What is reinforced

The eighth and the ninth Enneagram types have very little in common.

What contradicts itself

Basically, these two Enneagram types differ in all essential points:

1. Type 8 is active. Type 9 is passive.

2. Type 8 is aggressive. Type 9 is peace-loving.

3. Type 8 is industrious. Type 9 is lazy.

This list could be continued as long as you want.

Result

In the evolved form, this mixed type is kind-hearted and can assert himself. He sees things realistically and can respond to the needs of others.

In the unevolved form, he is aggressive, intimidating, cold-blooded, and also lazy, seeking only to find ways to use his advantage over others. He often exploits other people.

Frequency

This mixed type occurs relatively rarely.

8. Enneagram Exercises

In this chapter I want to introduce you to some exercises that will help you to better understand yourself, as well as the system of the Enneagram. Most of the exercises require that you have read the book up to this point, or that you are familiar with the nine types of the Enneagram.

In many cases, you need to give up your habitual way of perceiving your surroundings for the duration of the exercise, and identify yourself as much as possible with other Enneagram types. It may help you to imagine one person you know who corresponds to each type. Keep in mind that to each Enneagram type the world looks different. When this is clear to you, you will come closer to understanding that everyone is limited in his perceptions and in his way of reacting—just as you are.

On the other hand, you can, with sufficient attention, also discover traits of all the Enneagram types in yourself. Basically, we are all living different Enneagram types in different areas of our lives, even though most of the time, one or two Enneagram types determine most of our behavior.

EXERCISE: The Telling or Writing Down of Your Autobiography from the Viewpoint of Different Enneagram Points

You can write down your life story, or tell it to someone in various forms:

- criminal story
- fairy tale
- short story

or any other kind of literary form.

Try that and see which Enneagram type is the main character that is you! Check to see whether you act in different episodes as different Enneagram types.

Ask yourself the following questions:

- In which situations do I act as which Enneagram type?

- Which Enneagram type represents the basic structure of my actions and my view of the world?

According to Margaret Frings Keyes, each Enneagram type also has a certain style of speech and of narration.

- Enneagram Type 1 usually instructs with a preachy tone, and his story makes clear that he already knows what course it will take.

- In Type 2's story, advice and helping devices will play an important role (the figure of the servant in the English 19th century novel would be a case in point).

- Enneagram Type 3 is inclined to present him/herself as a superman/superwoman. He will always be the winner and the successful one in his story.

- Enneagram Type 4 will tell a sad emotional story, in which he depicts himself as an extraordinary personality. We find him there as artist, eccentric, or as a special outsider—those are the kinds of people he identifies with.

- Enneagram Type 5 will recite a smart story perfectly and in a scholarly way, and in it there will be extremely appropriate observations.

- Enneagram Type 6 will tend to tell of anxieties and persecutions. His story will be somewhat boring and conventional.

- Enneagram Type 7, on the other hand, will tell funny anecdotes or even such stories as in *1001 Nights*. He will only relate positive things (because he was always lucky and had a brilliant, often eventful, life).

- Enneagram Type 8 might love criminal stories or stories in which the events are not tame—commands and the enforcing of his will will be important for him.

- Enneagram Type 9 will recite slowly and in epic style (and maybe somewhat lasciviously). In contrast to Type 8, you can expect little action from him.

These Enneagram types, according to Margaret Frings Keyes, are of the classification of Ichazo, which deviates in some ways from the classification used by me in this book. For example, according to my classification:

- The first Enneagram type would write a story in which households or generally the economy plays a role.

- The second Enneagram type would shine through his story and want to please.

- The third Enneagram type would tell some kind of tall story.

- In the fourth and fifth types, I would agree with Margaret Frings Keyes.

- In the stories of the sixth Enneagram type, power fantasies would plan an important role.

- And at the last three Enneagram types, I would again agree with Margaret Frings Keyes.

After you have found your type, tell about your life again, but this time from the point of view of the Enneagram type that is your relief point (see pages 154–171). Take some time to do that and work out this new story in detail, being sure to focus on the relief Enneagram type. You will realize that it can be a lot of fun, and at the same time convey to you another perspective, which loosens up your habitual view.

Since all good things come in threes, you can, after that, describe your life from the perspective of the Enneagram type that represents your stress point.

Furthermore, you can examine from which *consciousness level* of the Enneagram you told your life or wrote it down. You can also change the consciousness level of the story, as you did with the Enneagram types. Tell your story once from the consciousness level that corresponds to your relief point, and another time from the consciousness that corresponds to your stress point.

Duration of this exercise

At least 30–60 minutes, perhaps longer—if need be, over several days (you can work out the individual stories on different days).

Advantage of this exercise

- It loosens your way of looking at the world and helps to dissolve what binds you to your Enneagram type.

- You get a deep feeling of contact with other people through your identification with another Enneagram type.

- You get a deep practical understanding of the system of the Enneagram.

Disadvantage of this exercise

- It is only suitable for people who have fun telling and/or writing stories.

- It takes quite a lot of time.

Expansion of this exercise

Other things to look at in this exercise: which

profession and life's goal you had in your youth, and which Enneagram type was expressed in that. Do you still live this part of you today, or do you live another Enneagram type?

Which Enneagram type was personified by important people in your life (parents, for example, or partner, etc.)?

EXERCISE: Drawing Your Own Life Path into the Enneagram

When you look at your resume—one that you have written for various job applications, you will notice that you showed—at different phases of your life and on different occasions—the characteristic features of different Enneagram types.

You can draw an Enneagram, and then enter at the individual Enneagram points, the section of your life and the time that goes with it. Let's take a look at one example:

Enneagram Point 1: Relatively smart about business as a pupil. Always has little jobs and income on the side (1956–1965).

Enncagram Point 2: Ambitious student who wants to help under-privileged people and create a nice world (1966–1971).

Enneagram Point 3: Successful therapist, who efficiently builds up his practice (1974–1980).

Enneagram Point 4: A short excursion into the artist's (and hippie) life, though in a subdued basic mood (1973).

Enneagram Point 5: Short time as a retreated scientific assistant at a university, accumulating a lot of knowledge without applying it creatively (1972).

Enneagram Point 6: Expressing that part of me that lets me persistently and determinedly work out an idea more and more clearly (from 1974 on).

Enneagram Point 7: More or less characterizes my entire life, as an undertone.

Enneagram Point 8: Lived out partially by me in a student movement (1968–1971).

Enneagram Point 9: Not occupied.

After you have recognized the Enneagram type in which you have lived in the different situations in your life, you can now enter—in another color—your development stages at the corresponding Enneagram point. For example:

Enneagram Point 1: Creating the pre-conditions for later life through learning in school and at the university (from 1956).

Enneagram Point 2: From 1965, purposeful collecting of information from books and through discussions with friends, through traveling and private studies, about what I would want to do later in my life.

Enneagram Point 3: A psychotherapist and a teacher enter my life and change my life path from a one-sided scientific orientation to a more artistic one. At the same time, I realize, through a serious illness and a near-death experience, how important my feelings are (1969–1972).

Enneagram Point 4: My feelings frighten me. I get confused. I think life is too hard and I long for my previous life. My therapy lets me recognize my negative sides and my false self-image (1972–1973).

I want to live completely differently and have doubts about the meaning of my work. I am moody, unstable, and long for the simple life that I led in the sixties. I begin to smoke. I leave my teacher (around 1990–1991).

Enneagram Point 5: As a Type 7, I decide that I do not want to suffer anymore and that I will now again, no matter what, orient myself emotionally toward happiness in my life (around 1974–1975).

A big crisis is caused by separation from a partner of many years. I fall into a depression-like irritability, retreat from all activities, and bury myself in my studies and exercises (1977–1982).

I go into psychotherapy again, in which I realize where I want to go (1991).

Enneagram Point 6: I meet a spiritual teacher, who accepts me as her student and teaches me consciousness exercises (from 1966).

I meet a woman who is important in my life, and at the same time a teacher with whom I work. I forget my depression and try to reach my life goal with perseverance (1983–1988).

Again I meet a teacher, whose work I now understand much more deeply, and who touches me emotionally. I begin to have a hunch that I am an emotional type, who became an intellectual through his parents (1992).

Enneagram Point 7: My feelings are not vacillating anymore. I succeed more and more often in using my negative feelings for self-recognition only, and not to live them. Through this, I am much more stable and grounded, and I have the feeling that I am leading the life that I want to lead (from 1975 on).

I live merrily and happily, and have the feeling that I have a lot of luck in life (1993).

Enneagram Point 8: I find that it makes sense to pass on my life experiences to others (from 1992 on).

Enneagram Point 9: Not reached.

Duration of this exercise

At least one hour, but you can also work at it for several days.

Advantage of this exercise

When you write down your life in this way, and refer it to the Enneagram, it has the following advantages:

- Recurring patterns become clear. In my example, you can see at once the difficulties of moving beyond the consciousness stage of the Enneagram Point 6. A closer look brought the realization that through a hidden rejection of the authority of the female teacher, this person relapsed here again and again. This makes itself noticeable in the loop of Enneagram points 4, 5, 6, 4, 5, 6, etc. Pay attention to such repetitions and try to understand them.

- You realize that a certain order is at the foundation of your life, which directs you spontaneously in many of your actions. In my example, it is the main orientation towards Enneagram Type 7 that gets this person to try again and again to create a happy life.

- It makes it clear to you where you stand exactly and how you could go on from there. In my example, the person could, for instance, get absorbed in the task of building up a center, as part of his practice as a therapist and spiritual teacher. Then, he would be able to help other people with his accumulated knowledge and experience. That would be an extension of the thoughts that were stated in the eighth Enneagram point. Here, new challenges would occur, with which this person could go through the Enneagram cycle again.

- It can be done without any great expenditure.

All in all, you can see that this exercise will create a high consciousness of the course of your life.

Disadvantage of this exercise

There is the danger that you can fool yourself in regard to your autobiography.

Expansion of this exercise

After you evaluate this exercise, ask yourself what you now still want to achieve. Then, following the connecting lines of the Enneagram, look at how you can get there. Ask yourself, at the same time, what you want to renounce the least.

Imagine just one aspect of life as you would like to have it, ideally. Would you then react just like your Enneagram type?

EXERCISE: Important People in my Life

Draw an Enneagram into which you enter all your female and male friends at their respective Enneagram points. Pay attention to accumulations, and at the types where there are no entries.

Looking at the Enneagram type to which most of your friends belong, ask yourself what the relationship is between that Enneagram type and your own. Ask yourself the same question about the Enneagram type that does not have any—or has the fewest entries.

Duration of this exercise

It depends how much time you take to do it. Normally, you can do the exercise in one evening. If you wish, you can restrict this observation to a certain time period. The smaller the time period, the faster the exercise can be done.

Advantage of this exercise

You get to know the dynamics of the Enneagram very well, by finding out which types your Enneagram type attracts, and to which types you are attracted.

Keep in mind that you probably, at different points in time, represented yourself as a different type.

Disadvantage of this exercise

The memory of old friends and lovers can very easily distort their image, and, as I said before, you cannot assume that people remain the same Enneagram type in all their dealings and at all times.

Expansion of this exercise

Basically, you would have to draw such an Enneagram for each Enneagram type that you represented in your life. If you have plenty of time, you can try to do that. It will make the dynamics of the Enneagram especially clear to you.

EXERCISE: Dream Symbols

Always, when I remember a dream, I make myself a list of the different symbols that occurred in the dream. There were, maybe, a cat, a car, a house, and some people. All these dream symbols—persons, animals, and objects—represent different egos of the dreamer, which are worth looking at.[27]

Ask yourself to which Enneagram type these dream symbols seem to belong. At the same time, ask yourself which Enneagram aspects are lived by you and which show up as "unlived aspects" in the dream.

Whatever shows up in the dream as a symbol often represents an unlived aspect of ourselves, which wants to be experienced. Or expressed the other way around, we often neglect the Enneagram aspects that characterize our dream symbols in our everyday life. That's why they make themselves noticeable in the dream.

Duration of the exercise

Maximum 15 minutes.

Advantage of the exercise

- It can be done easily.

- It helps us to understand our dreams more clearly.

- It also makes clear what is not being lived, and what we are not paying attention to, which is difficult to realize in any other way.

Disadvantages of the exercise

- It is tied to remembering dreams.

- Even though dreams have the tendency to set unlived and projected parts of us into scenes, not every dream symbol necessarily represents unlived parts of us.

EXERCISE: Evening Exercise

In the evening, with closed eyes, go backwards through the past day and pay attention to which ego was predominating. Ask yourself, which type was lived fully today. You can ask yourself, in addition, what alternative reaction possibilities might have been open to you?

The reason you run through the day backwards, is that in a chronological retrospective, we tend to rather mechanically survey the day, while in a backward look you change the perspective, and are able to make the day conscious to yourself in detail.

Duration of the exercise

Maximum of 10 minutes—after some practice, much faster.

Advantage of the exercise

- It can be done casily.

- It makes us recognize daily our restrictions, our stiffness, and our missed opportunities.

Disadvantages of the exercise

- It requires some discipline and concen-

tration—for example, making sure you don't drift off or fall asleep while doing it.

- In order to unfold its full effect, this exercise should be done daily. Only after you have begun to do it regularly will you derive the full benefit of it.

Expansion of this exercise

After you have gone through the day backwards, you can plan the next day. You can visualize it precisely, and picture how you would like to arrange it best. You might also imagine how you would approach the next day as another Enneagram type, which again clarifies your fixations and wishful thinking, and which dissolves action patterns that have gotten stuck.

EXERCISE: Creative Exercise

If, in the near future, you read a novel or see a film that appeals to you, make the effort of observing the way the novel or film was constructed in the light of the Enneagram.

Write down, first, which persons appear, and try to allocate them to the Enneagram types. Then look at the interactions of these people and try to understand them in accordance with the Enneagram.

The second step involves the development of the main character—or a person with whom you identify—to the Enneagram according to Gurdjieff. Can you figure out some of the nine consciousness steps here?

Duration of the exercise

Between 15 minutes and an hour.

Advantage of the exercise

This exercise helps you to understand the dynamics of the Enneagram and to use the Enneagram as an aid to the understanding of social structures and especially of social conflicts. It sharpens your view of your environment.

Disadvantage of the exercise

When dealing with longer novels and films, it is easy to lose the overview of the development of the characters.

Expansion of this exercise

I apply this exercise in my workshops with movie scriptwriters in the following altered form. You take an already completed script and determine which types appear in it, and whether they have been created correctly in regard to the Enneagram types. Then you look at the interaction of these types. It turns out that the more clearly a character corresponds to an Enneagram type, the more easily he can be recognized by the observer.

Since the Enneagram types, at the same time, represent archetypal images, with each creation the deep layers of the psyche of the observer are being addressed. Thereby, you can check whether the development of a person corresponds to the stages of the Enneagram. The more clearly a person portrays this development, the more clearly the person is represented to the spectator.

This exercise teaches how to use the Enneagram as an aid in developing a script. That means, in the last analysis, that the scriptwriter can learn to write a successful script through following the model of the Enneagram.

In all creative professions, such a utilization of the Enneagram can be learned.

Duration of the expanded exercise

The duration of the exercise depends for the most part on the size of the script.

Advantage of the expanded exercise

It gets easier with practice.

Disadvantage of this expanded exercise

It is of use only to people in creative professions.

GROUP ENNEAGRAM EXERCISES

EXERCISE: Finding Your Own Enneagram Type

Draw a large Enneagram in chalk on the floor (or you can instead stretch out some colored threads on the carpet and anchor them with pins).

First, each person, individually, walks along the lines of the Enneagram as concentratedly and consciously as possible. After that, all the members of the group go to the individual Enneagram points that correspond to them. When these positions have been taken up, and if everyone feels satisfied with his point, then the members of the group begin a conversation, each from his Enneagram point. If you want to say something about the content or in a manner that doesn't correspond to your own Enneagram point, then you need to move to the other Enneagram point and speak from there.

Duration of this exercise

It can be done as long as desired, but at least half an hour.

Advantages of the exercise

- You are able to absorb the Enneagram through what Gurdjieff calls the movement center.

- You become conscious of the various Enneagram types out of whose perspective you react. Through the physical change of position, you get an especially clear consciousness of the change in perspective.

Disadvantages of the exercise

As a pre-condition of this exercise, each member of the group must be familiar with the personality types of the Enneagram.

213

EXERCISE: An Experiment with Enneagram Types

This experiment calls for small groups. They must be combined of:

- types and their stress types, or

- types and their relief types

These groups are now given a small task, like, for example, painting a picture together or cooking a meal together that will be served to all the group members. Ask the members of the group at the beginning of this task to pay close attention to the upcoming conflicts, and to be aware as much as possible of every tension.

Duration of this exercise

The duration of the exercise depends on the task given the group, but it should not be any longer than one day.

Advantage of this exercise

- It shows us exactly our own shadow projections, because it is those that bother us in the other person.

- It reveals the tensions, but also the harmony that lies in the special mixture of the Enneagram stress and relief types.

- It makes us realize directly what the stress and relief type concretely means.

Disadvantage of this exercise

You need to know the group relatively well in order to be able to classify the members safely, according to stress or relief types. That means the Enneagram allocation of each group member must be clear, since otherwise you cannot identify the stress or relief types.

These exercises can be done more than once, and each time they will bring you many new realizations about yourself and the Enneagram. Except for the group exercises, you can perform these exercises very well alone or with a partner.

On the basis of these examples, you can also construct Enneagram exercises yourself, which are very specifically geared toward your needs. Give free rein to your creativity and experiment a little.

9. The Quintessence of the Enneagram at Work

Freedom and Decision

One big difficulty in doing work with the Enneagram lies in the fact that you have to construct Enneagrams yourself to fit your needs. I want, for example to begin a new work/job, and I want to clarify the process with the help of the Enneagram in order to get a better overview and understand what I can expect. Even though there are certain principles that we use to allocate the individual points to the Enneagram, we nevertheless live in a world that is not only externally determined, but also involves risk. Even though the world (which the Enneagram symbolizes) is ruled by laws, we still have possibilities for choice and selection. Therefore, how we allocate events and process sequences to the special Enneagram points is partially determined through the inner logic of the Enneagram. This logic determines, for example, that the first two Enneagram points have to do with the material pre-conditions of a process or with its preparation. The third Enneagram point characterizes an outside impulse or a new quality. The fourth and fifth Enneagram points occupy themselves with the organization of the pre-conditions toward the desired goal, and look at the execution of the required work. After that, again at Enneagram Point 6, an outside impulse follows. The last three Enneagram points indicate the goal or the realization of it.

On the other hand, the inner logic of the Enneagram allows certain freedoms. When we apply the Enneagram to a specific situation, we decide:

Which event do I allocate to which Enneagram point?

or

Which types have mixed here?

The Enneagram does not tell us how to break down a process to suit our needs. In short, applying the Enneagram (especially according to Gurdjieff) requires a great amount of creativity.

Enneagram Points and Their Meaning in Regard to Contents
Enneagram points 1 and 2: The material pre-conditions of a process The preparation of the process
Enneagram point 3: First, unconscious outside impulse New quality or level is reached
Enneagram points 4 and 5: Organization of the pre-conditions toward the goal The execution of the work
Enneagram points 6: Second conscious outside impulse New quality or level is reached
Enneagram points 7 and 8 The reaching of the goal The realization
Enneagram point 9 The transition to a new process

No matter how you apply it, the Enneagram will always show the consequences of our decisions and it will support us, while reducing our risks and perceiving ourselves, the other person, and the world more realistically. It helps us to see life as it really is, and, through that perspective, to give up the rigid—but comfortable—ideas we have about the world. Every time we do practical work with the Enneagram, we see the world with new eyes, which corresponds to the much praised beginner's spirit in Zen.

Never must a symbol like the Enneagram be applied rigidly; life is too complex. And a symbol is, after all, only a symbol. The Enneagram has to do with decisions, and decisions always raise the question of freedom and selection, for which there is no absolute answer.

The Nature of the Enneagram Work

Enneagram work involves a tension between ties to cosmic laws and the freedom of decision. Gurdjieff's student John Godolphin Bennett drew attention to the fact that it is possible to escape from even karmic law, since one can escape from every fixed law.[28] Well-known dramas like Goethe's *Faust* and Ibsen's *Peer Gynt* always end with the hero escaping punishment or, in the last analysis, justice. World literature reminds us continually of our relative freedom of decision.

In his book about risk and freedom, Bennett draws attention to the fact that the Yezidis,[29] in whose religion zoroastical elements survived, believe:

"that indeed the behavior of the human being in this world is of importance, and that his engagement on the one or on the other side can influence the final result."[30]

Every person has the freedom to choose the forces of the light or of the darkness. Which of the two sides finally asserts itself in the world depends on every ever so small decision. Our universe is a structure that requires the intelligent collaboration of the human being. The core of Gurdjieff's teachings lies in the fact that the human being can reach his self-realization only through conscious service at the creation, just as the creation gets its realization only through the cooperation of the consciously acting human being.

The Enneagram makes it clear to us that we represent a part of a larger unity—indeed, that we are a vital element in the cosmos. With this viewpoint, Gurdjieff has, among other things, anticipated our new ecological awareness. He realized, at the beginning of the century, that an important and active role in the future balance of the biosphere falls to humankind. An ecologically sensible way of behavior on the part of the human being can be considered an important service for nature.

This is for me the quintessence of Enneagram work. We are connected to everything, which the lines of the Enneagram clarify, and at the same time, macrocosmic laws are reflected in the microcosm of the human being. Only because of that, can we refer the Enneagram to the human being, to the planets, to light phenomena like the colors, to sounds, and, in the last analysis, to all processes (the way things work) on earth. All that is subject to the same laws that the Enneagram symbolizes. And we were given the latitude to deal with these laws freely. We are, though, largely dependent on the consequences of our actions, even if we can sometimes appear to escape from them.

The Intelligent Enneagram— A Synthesis

I want to present, in this last section of my workbook for the Enneagram, my view of the Enneagram that connects the two "hostile brothers"—Ichazo's concepts and the process model. This synthesis connects/combines a psychological character study (personality types) with a therapy model (the dynamic, process-oriented view). This "intelligent Enneagram," represents at the same time—as shown in this book—an astonishingly exact model for interpreting the world, loosening former Enneagram research and application out of its rigidity. In the last years, more and more criticism of the idea of personality types could be heard, since the rigid application of these teachings departs from reality and becomes a matter of fiction.

In reality, we can easily see that the nine types, which the Enneagram assumes, mix in many ways. The weaknesses of the rigid concept of types, as it is currently used, are the "children's sicknesses" of the Enneagram work. They can be eliminated by anyone with many years of experience doing practical applications with the Enneagram.

I want to summarize in a condensed fashion, how the Enneagram as presented here offers a synthesis of the different applications and considerations regarding it.

The triangle of the Enneagram reflects the common laws of each process. The hexagon, on the other hand, reflects the individual structure of the process. If you refer to these two basic statements of the concept of personality types, you can say that the basic archetypal structures correspond to the triangle points, and that the hexagon points are comparable to the archetypal images. That means, in the sense of C. G. Jung, that the triangle points represent basic perceptions of structures, while the hexagon points are images derived from those basic structures. Therefore, the triangle points grasp the types on a deeper level than do the hexagon points, which represent a level once removed.

If you belong to a type at a certain time and in a certain situation—let's say, for example, to the Enneagram Type 1—then it is important to move first toward Enneagram Point 7 (the relief point) in order for the individual to reach self-perfection (individuation) and achieve greater completeness. From the seventh Enneagram point, he needs to move in the next relief direction—to the fifth Enneagram point—and from there to the next, the eighth, and then via the second to the fourth Enneagram point. That is precisely the path of individuation, understood as the path to completeness.

The 5 Steps to Completeness

From
$$1 \rightarrow 7$$
$$7 \rightarrow 5$$
$$5 \rightarrow 8$$
$$8 \rightarrow 2$$
$$2 \rightarrow 4$$

In the same way, all the other types of the hexagon (Enneagram types 2, 4, 5, 7, and 8) get five stages to reach completeness.

This path through the Enneagram creates consciousness by expanding the viewpoint of the searching person. It helps him to perceive life through more perspectives than before. It also gives him the ability to take on the visual angle of the other Enneagram types. Thus, it is not the goal to freeze in one personality type, but to reach a mobile viewpoint. Conscious advancement means to develop oneself further in the Enneagram and to expand the possibilities and degrees of freedom.

The 2 Steps to Completeness

From
$$3 \rightarrow 6$$
$$6 \rightarrow 9$$

If you look at one of the three triangle points, the third Enneagram point, for example, you will see that development to completeness can be achieved in only two steps. He must enrich his Type 3 perspective with the Type 6 and the Type 9 perspectives in order to achieve completeness.

So, the different levels lie in the fact that hexagon types perfect themselves in five

217

steps, and triangle types in only two, since they reflect the more basic level of the personality structure.

Just as an Enneagram type becomes richer in the individuation process by assimilating the features of the other types and winning more freedom, so does the person's way of reacting change from situation to situation. The dynamics are created not only because you expand in the individuation process by changing the ways you look at the things of the different Enneagram types, but also because you can be different types on different levels. The reason for this is that you manifest different consciousnesss stages in different situations. Some forms of therapy have pointed out for a long time that, in some situations, the parents speak out of the mouth of the child. In Gurdjieff's sense, we could say that the human being lives out of three centers—the intellectual, the emotional, and the movement center. According to my observation, you can—on the level of the movement center, for example—react as a completely different type than on the level of the intellectual or emotional centers.

This is why all wisdom teachings stress that the person should develop himself on all three levels harmonically. In Yoga, we find the idea expressed that you need to let your energies rise evenly in the three "Yoga-nerves": Ida (female path), Pingala (male path), and Sushumna (neutral path).

In the same way, the person needs to develop his consciousness evenly in physical, intellectual, and emotional ways. Unfortunately, our development runs unevenly in this respect, which is reflected in our reacting to different situations as different Enneagram types. The path of individuation must be run through on all three levels, so that the person eventually reaches an even development and a harmony of body, spirit, and soul. I know, for example, a child that reacts actively on a physical level and is highly performance-motivated, like Type 3. He gets his self-confidence from his physical achievements. But on the intellectual level, this child resembles Type 9. He is rather lazy and shows a tendency to mental sloth. We all have the tendency to exhibit different behavior on different levels, and therefore we must work through each level in our own way.

At this point, we can see clearly the connection between the rigid personality types and the dynamic process-oriented model of the Enneagram. In the Enneagram as a process-oriented model, we stride ahead from point to point through the mastering of a situation. That means that we expand our consciousness step-by-step. In the process of coming to understand a situation, our Enneagram type changes. It is immediately understandable that in a continued process, the Enneagram type must change, since it was originally determined by views of the world, strategies of problem-solving, and ways of reacting. In order to see a situation differently or more productively, and to be able to solve it, it is important to loosen up the tight and rigid way of looking at things that belonged to the original Enneagram type, and expand it with those of another Enneagram type.

Let's look at this from another perspective. I recognize in myself the fixations and wishful thinking of a certain Enneagram type through my occupation with the concept of personality types. The process model of the Enneagram gives me a hint as to how I can open myself up in order to win greater freedom. So, my recognition of the reactions of the type I now personify would be standing at Enneagram Point 1 in the process model. The loosening up of my fixated way of looking at things and reacting would be the goal of my Enneagram work at the ninth Enneagram point. At that point, I would gain the way of looking at things of another Enneagram point.

Thus, the process model explains how you can change your Enneagram type and stride ahead from Enneagram type to Enneagram type, and thus widen your consciousness.

While in my earlier publications regarding the Enneagram, I acted rather as a critic of rigid Enneagram use, I see today, in addition, that not only the teaching of personality types, but also the process-oriented side is in danger of being reduced to a schematic use. It is easier to understand and apply things rigidly, but when you do, they by no means correspond to reality.

I begin to understand why it has been that the Enneagram was passed on only orally from teacher to pupil. In the last analysis, we can only personally convey the dynamic, "intelligent" use of the Enneagram by showing a pupil in a real-life situation where neither the type nor the development point in the Enneagram are rigidly fixed. The dynamic side of the individual development points reveal that in everyday life there are different ways to look at things and different ways of behaving in regard to a situation. How we subdivide the process into nine Enneagram points—which means nine development steps—depends on our creativity and perception.

There are always different possibilities for understanding a process in the Enneagram. Let's have a look at how we can expand our way of looking at things by assimilating the way of looking at things of another Enneagram type.

The first possibility of understanding this process in the Enneagram:

The way of looking at things and reacting of our present Enneagram type corresponds to the first Enneagram point.

Our growing uneasiness with this tight way of looking at things corresponds to the second Enneagram point.

At Enneagram Point 3, an outside impulse occurs, which reveals our rigidity in such a way that we cannot deny it is a shortcoming.

At Enneagram Points 4 and 5, we suffer from the recognition of our restrictions, but we do not know yet how we can change. Tension builds up inside us, which prepares us to get out of this rigid character armor.

At the second shock point, Enneagram Point 6, it is often a teacher, a course, or a book such as this one that shows the way to step out of our limitation.

At Enneagram Point 7, we then have gained a new view of the world, which, at the eighth Enneagram point can be transformed through taking action.

At the ninth Enneagram point, we will go on to expand our way of looking at things all over again.

The second possibility of understanding this process in the Enneagram:

Again, the way of perceiving and reacting of the present Enneagram type corresponds to the first Enneagram point.

The second Enneagram point makes it clear to us how rigidly and one-sidedly we behave.

This shock makes us take on, at the third Enneagram point, an expansion of our way of looking at the world and reacting. We leave the tightness of our original ways of looking and enrich it by adding the perceptions of another Enneagram point.

At the fourth Enneagram point, new difficulties arise with this new way of looking at the world.

At the fifth Enneagram point, it becomes clear that even this new way of seeing is too restricted.

At the sixth Enneagram point, we again change our point of view, in order to

219

realize, at the eighth Enneagram point, that this new way of reacting is still too limited and that we have to widen our horizon.

At the ninth Enneagram point, we enrich our way of looking at the world with that of another Enneagram point.

Both possibilities of understanding the individuation process are valid; they merely emphasize different aspects of the process.

Everyone knows that it is very different looking at a process at its start than seeing it from the state of consciousness of your goal. When you change your state of consciousness, you often see new possibilities of the division of a process. The more possibilities you see for division, the more conscious you are of this process and the more easily you can use it creatively and productively.

Let's have a look at our body in the Enneagram: The physical aspects can be allocated to the first two points (Enneagram Points 1 and 2), in which it is stressed that the physical needs are the basic ones onto which all the others are built. This starting point, though, is inclined to classify the body as inferior. Furthermore, we could allocate to the body Enneagram points 7 and 8, and emphasize that the formation of higher consciousness is only possible in keeping with the body.

Both starting points are "correct," because we get into our inner world only through our own body, which at the same time represents the foundation of all our needs.

Last, but not least, I want to emphasize that our work to change our consciousness has to be looked at under the visual angle of the Enneagram. The highest stage of the application of the Enneagram, about which I can only guess—and at which my teacher sometimes grants me a brief glance—represents Enneagram Point 9. With this point, you leave the system of the Enneagram. Here you have reached a stage of consciousness on which you realize that a model is only a model. The Enneagram represents a map of our consciousness, which, like a road map, is not the territory itself. The model of the Enneagram helps us to perceive more consciously the complex reality in which we live. Once this recognition takes place, the model should be given up, not only because the lowest step of the Enneagram is its use as a set of personality types, but also because the dynamic Enneagram, would, in the last analysis, rob us of mobility if we held onto it. On the level of consciousness work, this corresponds to the understanding that we need to give up a teacher and a system after a certain time in order to be able to continue to develop. Thus, says Henri Tracol, the sculptor and president of the Gurdjieff Society in Paris, "Since there is nothing in us or outside of us that does not change, it is absurd wanting to put this movement into rigid concepts."[31]

The Enneagram teaches us to see each of our actions in a larger connection. It shows us that we are an important little wheel in the cosmos. Therefore, it is practical for us to have a tool like the Enneagram with which we can determine the results of our actions.

The Enneagram can be seen as a guidepost to freedom, but we must not let a guidepost block the view toward freedom. When the Enneagram makes itself independent and dominates the human being with its rigid forms, it turns us into the mechanical robots it originally wanted to save us from. If you see the Enneagram only as a rigid model of personality types, then you are using it in a way that belies its original meaning.

The quintessence of the Enneagram work lies for me in the connection of the personality types with the observation and analyses of processes and social courses. This aspect of the Enneagram work is seldom emphasized. I do hope that, with this workbook, I have opened up a more exciting and useful way of dealing with the Enneagram.

Notes

1. Carl Gustav Jung, *The Collected Works of C. G. Jung* (Princeton University Press).

2. Bruno Martin, *Handbook of the Spiritual Paths: A Journey of Discovery* (Basel 1993).

3. P. D. Ouspensky, *In Search of the Miraculous: Fragments of an Unknown Teaching* (New York, 1965).

4. Helen Palmer, *The Enneagram: Understanding Yourself and Others in Your Life* (San Francisco, 1991).

5. Strictly speaking, there are five phases of sexual development according to Sigmund Freud, but no type is allocated to the latent period.

6. Klausbernd Vollmar, *The Secrets of Enneagrams: Mapping the Personality* (Dorset, 1993).

7. Boris Mouravieff, *Gnosis: Esoteric Cycle (Study and Commentaries on the Esoteric Tradition of Eastern Orthodoxy: Volume 3*, Praxis Institute, 1993).

8. Madhu Khanna, *The Great Yantra Book: The Tantric Symbol of Cosmic Unity* (London, 1994).

9. Classic astronomy, as well as astrology, works with the concept of octaves. That means that the planets beyond Saturn are seen as being a higher vibration of Mercury, Venus, and Mars. Uranus is the octave of Mercury, Neptune the octave of Venus, the Pluto the octave of Mars.

10. To mention only the most important Enneagram tests: Markus Becker, *The Enneagram Type Test*. Richard Rohr and Andreas Ebert, *Experiences with the Enneagram*. Don Richard Riso, *Discovering Your Personality Type: The Enneagram Questionnaire*. Margaret Frings Keyes, *Enneagram and Partnership: A Workbook for Individuals, Couples and Groups*. Klausbernd Vollmar, *The Enneagram*.

11. Lois Bourne, *Experiences of a Witch*.

12. The mathematician Kurt Godel proved that a completely closed and in itself consistent system cannot exist. That also applies to the Enneagram, which shows three special points at which outside impulses have an effect on the system.

13. You can learn conscious dreaming with the help of the affirmation, "This night I am conscious in the dreams that I dream." For detailed instructions, see James J. Donahoe's *The Art af Dreaming* and Patricia Garfield's *Creative Dreaming*.

14. Klausbernd Vollmar, *The Enneagram*.

15. Henrich E. Benedikt, *Die Kabbala als Judische-Christlicher Ein Weihungsweg*.

16. It is no coincidence that Gurdjieff in his seeming autobiographical novel *Meetings with Remarkable Men* describes nine people who have influenced him substantially. Therefore, it is striking that at the points that jut out of the Enneagram—the shock points 3 and 6—the priest Bogatschevsky and the prince Juri Lubowedsky are described. The chapter about Bogatschevsky is about morals, and was supposed to have formed Gurdjieff's opinion that a valid moral always exists. In the chapter on Lubowedsky, which is strictly symbolic, Gurdjieff at last finds the secret cloister of the Sarmoun Brotherhood, and is introduced to their secret doctrines, and especially into the Enneagram and the Movements. The number Nine and the structure of the Enneagram do not play an important role, however, in *Meetings with Remarkable Men*.

17. Richard Rohr/Andreas Ebert, *Das Enneagram: Die neun Gesichter der Seele* (Munich, 1989).

18. Eliane Ganem, , *Bluten der Erkenntnis* (Wessobrunn, 1993). There are many parallels between this book and my allocation of the Bach flowers to the individual chakras.

19. Johannes Fiebig, *The Lowe in uns* (Konigsfurt, 1991).

20. Caroline A. F. Rhys Davids, translator and editor, *Stories of Buddha: Being Selections from the Jataka* (Dover Publications, New York, 1989). The quoted story is also known by the title, "The Jataka of the Sandy Road."

21. In my Enneagram workshops, Type 5s, and somewhat less frequently Type 7s, are always most strongly represented.

22. Sicuteri, Roberto, *Astrologie und Mythos. Mythen und Symbole im Spiegel der Tiefenpsychologie* (Freiburg, 1983).

23. Jung, op cit.

24. Rohr and Ebert, op cit.

25. Don Richard Riso, *Discovering Your Personality Type: The Enneagram Questionnaire* (Houghton Mifflin, N.Y. 1992).

26. Jung, op cit.

27. Klaus Vollmar, *Little Giant Encyclopedia of Dream Symbols* (Sterling, N.Y. 1997).

28. John Godolphin Bennett, *Risiko und Freiheit* (Sudergellersen, 1983).

29. The Yezidis, also called Yazides, are the followers of a religion of the Kurds, organized according to tribes that were named after Umayyades-Caliph Yazid lst (680–683). Though they never said the name of the devil, other Muslims called them devil-worshipers, and they were persecuted as Shismatics.

30. Bennett, op cit.

31. Henri Tracol, *The Taste for Things That Are True* (Shaftsbury, 1994). Essays and talks by a pupil of G. I. Gurdjieff.

If you are interested in seminars, workshops, courses and lectures about the Enneagram, please write to the following address:

Klausbernd Vollmar
Rhu-Sila
Cley next the Sea
Holt
Norfolk NR 25 7 UD
Great Britain

About the Author

KLAUS VOLLMAR is a psychologist and healing practitioner. He was born November 22, 1946, in Remscheid, Germany. After finishing the Abitur (high school degree), he completed studies in German, linguistics, and philosophy. A lecturer at the Goethe Institute in Finland, he received a scholarship from the Canada Council. He then studied educational psychology, learned Jungian depth-psychology techniques, and became a manager of youth advisory boards in Amsterdam and Solingen. A pupil of Freifrau von Dr. Olga von Ungern-Sternberg and the Schamane Black Horse Chavers, he was a member of an English Gurdjieff group for many years. Since 1980, he has worked independently as a psychotherapist, seminar leader and author. He lives in England and lectures and conducts seminars on the Enneagram, dream interpretation, and chakras work in Europe and North America.

He has written many books on such subjects as the Enneagram, dreams, the chakras, colors, travel, channeling, and autogenous training.

Index